Fishing the Headwaters of the Missouri

Norman Strung

Illustrations by C. W. "Wally" Hansen

Mountain Press Publishing Company
Missoula 1980

Library of Congress Cataloging in Publication Data

Strung, Norman.
  Fishing the headwaters of the Missouri.

  1. Fishing — Montana — Guide-books.   2. Trout
fishing — Montana — Guide-books.
3. Fishing — Missouri River — Guide-books.   I. Title.
SH517.S87   799.1'2'097861   80-12127
ISBN 0-87842-123-8 (pbk.)

MOUNTAIN PRESS PUBLISHING CO.
283 West Front Street • Missoula, Montana 59801
(406) 728-1900

To Richie Dougherty,
who loves the Missouri Headwaters as I do,
and who always catches the most fish.

Acknowledgements

To C.J.D. Brown, for use of illustrations from his book *Fishes of Montana,* published by Big Sky Books, Montana State University, Bozeman.

To Jim Harrison, Baldy Mountain Sports Shop, Dillon: John Spencer, Four Rivers Sport Shop, Twin Bridges: Bill Peck, The Alpine Sports Shop, Whitehall: and Phil Wright, The Complete Fly Fisher, Wisdom, for sharing their knowledge of the Jefferson drainage.

To Dick Vincent, Montana Department of Fish, Wildlife and Parks, for use of the thermographs of the Madison River he so painstakingly assembled.

To hundreds of nameless fishermen, who in ways large and small, contributed to the knowledge amassed within the pages that follow.

Introduction

The headwaters of the Missouri represent the greatest trout fishing opportunity in the world, and that is no idle boast. Nowhere else is there an equivalent concentration of rivers, streams, and lakes of such reknown and quality.

In any discussion of the world's most famous trout streams, one hears names like the Test and the Beaverkill, Chile, Argentina, and New Zealand's South Island. But one will also hear Montana: the Madison and the Yellowstone, the Big Hole, and the Gallatin.

Chile, New Zealand, England, and New York are thousands of miles apart. Every lake and stream in the Missouri headwaters is less than a day's drive from its most distant neighbor.

Proximity isn't the region's only recommendation. Few places boast of a greater variety of coldwater gamefish, a greater variety of habitat, or more fish, be the yardstick numbers, inches, or pounds. Within this watershed there are hundreds of miles of rivers, thousands of miles of streams, and hundreds of thousands of surface acres of sparkling lakes, each loaded with natural populations of brook, brown, or rainbow trout, cutthroat, golden trout, or grayling.

The region is as vast as the fishing opportunities: over 10,000 square miles of prairie, valleys, canyons, hills, and mountains. It is a profile of enormity that whets the appetite, staggers the imagination, and poses a natural question: where does one begin?

Fishing the Headwaters of the Missouri addresses that question.

Each chapter deals with one facet of the jewel known as the Missouri Headwaters: the tackle a fisherman will need, the rivers that drain it, the streams that feed the rivers, and the lakes that feed the streams. There are maps indicating key access areas, floating statistics, illustrations and descriptions of all native fishes, and bits of information and local color that are of interest to fisherfolk; in short, this is a personal guide to the legendary waters of south-central Montana.

I feel honor-bound, however, to point out what this book isn't. It is not a guide to the best fishing holes. I do know a rock somewhere on the Madison River where I can catch a dozen big trout any day of the summer. And a little stream where I always fill my creel with brook trout up to 12 inches and rainbows up to 15, all of them taken on a #12 Royal Wulff.

They are discoveries of mine, personal and sweet, and to reveal them would be to destroy them. Know that they are out there though, and countless places like them. All it takes to find them is a little knowledge, a little time, and the willingness to venture beyond the road-ends. The time and work are up to the individual. It is my sincere hope that this book will provide the necessary knowledge.

Norman Strung
Bozeman, Montana

Contents

Tackle

To some extent, tackle amounts to an expression of style. I know that mine is. Still, I have come to the conclusion that certain items of equipment are uniquely suited to fishing the Missouri Headwaters.

Of course, you can get by with your favorite 7½-foot cane fly rod and a pair of hip boots. You could even take trout on an old bamboo pole, or a handline for that matter. But the more perfectly you match your gear to the conditions you will face, the better chance you will have of tempting and taking the fish you are after.

To that end, the following represents a list of equipment I have come to lean on, with a few of the reasons why I favor it. Use it as a guide tempered by your personal likes and dislikes.

FLY FISHING TACKLE

Rods

I have found an 8- to 9-foot graphite rod to be the workhorse for both rivers and lakes.

The reason for such a long rod is reach, period. The longer you can cast, the more fish you will catch. With the exception of small streams, Western fishing is not intimate fishing. Rivers stretch a hundred yards from bank to bank, and there is plenty of room for a back cast. Waters are swift and deep, and there are many stations that are unsafe or impossible to approach with waders. If you can handle a long line, you can reach them with a cast, tempting the trout of deeper water.

A long rod is also the prescription for lake fishing. Trout in regional lakes like to follow a nymph for long distances. Should they be feeding on top, you will put them down if you approach them too closely. Here, too, the reach of a long rod is essential.

I recommend graphite over cane or glass because it is lighter and more powerful than either. Your wrist will appreciate that lightness after you fish all day with a long rod, and the extra power of graphite will add critical feet to each cast. Graphite rods are also adaptable to a wider range of line weights and tapers than other rods, so you aren't burdened with extras, or with decisions about when to use which rod.

The line weight to choose? The heaviest that you can comfortably handle during a full day of casting. Again, heavy line is the medium for long casts. My personal choice is a seven-weight rod that I load with eight-weight line. More about that unusual combination in a moment.

At the other end of the spectrum, I recommend you also take the 4½- to 6-foot "flea" rod. One of the most overlooked, and hence hottest, fishing opportunities in the Missouri headwaters is small stream fishing. Creeks you can jump across often hold trophy trout that have never felt a hook. Many of these watercourses are canopied by over-story, or pinched tight by overhanging branches. A short rod is the most practical way to fish them.

If you are a spin fisherman as well as a fly fisherman, here's a tip. Buy a parabolic action ultra-light spinning rod, with a movable reel seat. They are perfectly suited to fly fishing and amount to two rods in one.

If you are an equipment freak, you'll probably want to have more than these two rods available. Yes, you'll be able to use your favorite 7½-foot cane on the upper reaches of the major rivers, but you'll find that a long rod or a short rod will suffice on 95% of the rivers, lakes, and streams of the Missouri Basin.

Lines

I carry three lines with me: a floating line, a floating line with a sink-tip, and a floating line with a high density sink-tip. All three lines have weight-forward tapers.

With these three lines, I can work top, mid, and bottom feeding zones. I prefer the weight-forward taper because it casts the farthest. I also recommend that you buy line that is one weight heavier than your rod. It will cast farther than the prescribed weight line, and it will probably improve your casting as well. With this heavier line, the moment of loading is easier to feel on your back cast, so you get maximum recoil from the shaft.

Why not sinking line? Because I have become convinced that the swift currents of these rivers elevate sinking line through drag. I find that a high-D sink-tip gets just as deep as full sinking line, and it mends much more easily. If you plan to do a lot of lake fishing, or to dredge the deeper holes of the lower reaches of the Jefferson, Missouri, or Yellowstone for browns, you will find a use for sinking line. But with these exceptions, you will probably find a sinking line more of a burden than a blessing.

Reels

Your fly reel should have interchangeable arbors, loaded with the aforementioned lines. It should also be capable of holding 30 yards of 20-pound test monofilament backing.

Conditions can change quickly. Trout may switch from bottom to top feeding patterns and back in a matter of moments. With interchangeable arbors, rather than individual reels, you can carry the extra line more compactly and comfortably, and be prepared to meet any changes in mood quickly. The backing is extra insurance that you won't lose the trout of a lifetime. The heaviest fish to come out of the Missouri Headwaters was a 29½ pound brown, caught in 1964.

Leaders

Bring a selection of 9-foot leaders, with 2X to 6X tippets. The major tributaries of the Missouri are usually cloudy to milky in color, even during low water periods. When this condition exists, use the heaviest leader practical. On these waters, I seldom fish with anything lighter than a 4X tippet.

Small streams and lakes, on the other hand, are commonly clear, so when I fish them, 5X or 6X tippets grace the tail of my leader.

You will also save a few dollars if you carry spools of straight leader material with you, from 2X to 6X. When fly changes or wind knots work their way into the thicker portions of your leader, just barrel-knot additional material to the end, rather than tying onto a whole new leader.

Flies

Western fly patterns would make a book. If you buy your flies, you're best off to purchase them locally, as many patterns are unique to an area. If you are a tier, the following are standards:

• **Dries** — #12 to #16 Royal Wulff, Goofus Bug, Irresistable, Elk Hair Caddis, Adams, Light Cahill, Mosquito; #6 to #10 Hoppers, Fluttering Salmon Fly.

• **Nymphs** — #12 to #16 Hare's Ear, Muskrat Caddis, Montana Nymph; #6 to #10 Bitch Creek, Green and Brown Wooly Worm, Girdle Bug.

• **Streamers** — #4 to #10 Muddler, White, Black and Yellow Maribou Muddler, Spuddler, Spruce, Royal Coachman Streamer, Big Horn Special.

Miscellaneous

• **Fly Dry** — bring both silicone spray and dessicant power. Insect films are common, and they'll sink a fly like soap unless you use this stuff.

• **Leader Sink** — will be necessary on the clearer lakes

and spring creeks. Use it just on the last foot of leader, or it will drag your fly down.

- **B-B Split Shot** — with this, there's no need for the agony of weighted flies. You just weight the leader instead.
- **Hackle Scissors** — for trimming leaders and ratty-looking flies, and turning dries and wets into nymphs.

There are other items of equipment you should have on or about you when fishing the Missouri Headwaters, but they're applicable to spin lure and bait fishermen as well. I'll discuss this equipment in a moment, but first let me address these two other segments of the fishing fraternity.

SPINNING WITH LURES

Rods

The all-around rod for the Missouri Headwaters is a 7- to 7½-foot fast action rod, with a light tip. A movable rather than a fixed reel seat is also preferable. You will also gain some advantages if the rod has an outsized butt guide.

As in fly casting, a long spinning rod gives you the greatest reach — reach that allows you to cast into water that would otherwise be denied you. A movable reel seat allows you to adjust to a wide weight range of spinning lures. By moving your reel forward or back, you can arrive at a perfect balance between rod, reel, and lures from ¼-ounce to ⅝-ounce. At one time or another, you will use both small and large lures. An outsized butt guide gives you greater reach too, and it promotes accuracy by regulating friction between line and guide.

If you enjoy small stream fishing, carry a 4½- to 5-foot ultra-lite spinning rod, with a movable reel seat. These rods match the size of the stream you'll be fishing, and they are best for casting the tiny lures that small-stream trout want.

A parabolic action is in order, because ultralite lures don't set up enough resistance to a rod shaft to put a fast tip to work. A parabolic action "bends to the corks" without a heavy lure, and thus propels dime-sized jewelry more efficiently.

Reels

Pick a standard weight (6- to 8-ounce) open faced spinning reel, with easily interchangeable spools, as a mate to the 7-foot rod. Use two spools, one loaded with 8-pound test line, and one with 6-pound line. Use the 8-pound line in snaggy water. It is stout enough to wrench most hooks free of entanglements. Use the 6-pound test in open water; it will cast a lure further than 8-pound line.

Pack an ultra-lite reel (4- to 6-ounce) with changeable spools, too. Load one spool with 4-pound test, one with 2-pound test. I would recommend that you bring this reel, even if you don't bring an ultra-lite rod. When extreme distance-casting is required (and it will be required if you fish lakes), you can toss a ½-ounce lure a country mile with 4-pound line and a 7½-foot rod. 2-pound test could conceivably be required in clear spring creeks and high mountain lakes, and the drag on a standard weight reel usually isn't critical enough to handle it. This gossamer line also tosses tiny ultra-lite lures the best.

High-quality ball-bearing snapswivels in the smallest size you can find are essential equipment. Western rivers are swift and set a spoon or spinner to whirling. If you don't use a snapswivel, line twist will sentence you to hours under trees undoing bird's nests in your mono.

Lures

If you can't find these brands at home, you can buy them locally:

¼-ounce Mepps and Panther Martins in silver and gold. Pearl Dardevle.

⅜-ounce Mepps, Panther Martins, hammered metal

spoons; Doty Raiders in silver and gold. Fluorescent and gold Wonderlures.

Thomas Cyclone and Thomas Bouyant in silver and brass. Pearl Dardevle, Fishscale Roostertail.

½-ounce Rapala diving plugs in silver and gold. Little Jewel, silver and gold; Krocodile and Kamlooper, fluorescent red and gold.

⅝-ounce hammered metal spoons in silver, gold, brass, and gold with a fluorescent stripe. Mepps, Panther Martin in silver and gold.

This selection should provide you the lures to fish all varieties of rivers, lakes and streams, and to reach all feeding zones. The suggested reels and rods, in various combinations, will prove perfectly suited to their different weights.

SPINNING WITH BAIT

You can always fish garden hackle with a fly rod or a standard spinning rod, but to my way of thinking, bait fishing is a far more sophisticated procedure than put-a-worm-on-a-hook and wait. The following equipment is my choice to satisfy the delicate nuances of advanced bait fishing techniques:

• A 7 or 7½-foot parobolic action rod with a movable reel seat and outsized butt guide. The same rules of reach hold true here as for spinning with lures. A parabolic or "soft" action rod allows you to lob a soft bait without snapping it off the hook. The "noodle" or "bicycle" rods popular with steelheaders are satisfactory too.

• A standard weight spinning reel, with easily changed spools, loaded with 8- and 4-pound test fluorescent line. The two spools allow you to handle light and heavy baits. The florescent feature makes it easier to follow your line with drift-fishing, and thus to identify a nibbling fish.

• Extra spools of 8- and 4-pound test leader material. I am

not sold on the proposition that fish cannot see fluorescent line; hence I barrel-know two feet of conventional mono leader to it.

• B-B, #14, and cannonball split shot. In moving water, you will have to weight your bait so it just scrapes bottom, and you will encounter flow velocities of 1 to 8 knots in the West. Some combination of these weights will match any of these conditions.

• A clear plastic casting bubble. With it, you can still-fish, float a neutral-bouyancy bait just off the bottom, or fish a large, adult fly or terrestrial on top when the trout are rising.

• Hooks: #4, 6, 8, and 10 baitholder hooks. Double needle sculpin hooks, #4 and #8. 2X Fine dry fly hooks, #12 and #16. The baitholder hooks will suffice to spear whatever size worm it is that the trout want. The sculpin hooks are best for this bait. The fly hooks will fit any number of nymphs you dredge up from the river bottom, and if you wish to fish a large adult on top, they are not so heavy as to sink it.

• Miscellaneous: a 2'x2' patch of cheesecloth to catch bait.

SUPPORT EQUIPMENT

Whatever fishbait graces the end of your line, it won't be enough to satisfy the needs of a serious fisherman. There's a considerable amount of additional equipment that will put you closer to your quarry.

• **Chest Waders.** These will prove to be nearly as important as a rod and reel to your fishing. They open up highways of water that are beyond the reach of anglers tied to the bank, and in many cases, they are the key to stream access. If you are buying a new pair of waders, look into Red Ball's "Flyweight" system. The waders weigh a mere 12 ounces, they roll up into a tight ball, they're tough, and they're cool and comfortable to wear. Wade wet? Yes, it's a possibility on hot days; but morning and evening water will be cool to downright cold. Hip waders are useful only on small streams. They're too short to get around on large rivers.

• **Carpeted Wader Boots.** The rocks that pave the bottom of the Missouri's tributaries are like greased cannonballs. Add the usual swift current, and you'll encounter a problem that ranges from an annoyance to a real danger. You'll take most of the slide out of those slick rocks if you'll cover the sole of your wading boot or shoe with felt, indoor/outdoor carpeting, abrasive grit, or some similar medium.

• **Wading Staff.** If you commonly use a wading staff, you will want one of the Missouri headwaters. I don't normally carry one, but there have been times when I wished I had.

• **Landing Net.** Whether you plan to keep fish or not, carry a small landing net. They are kind to fish you wish to release in that they shorten the exhausting period of battle and afford a surer, less-injurious grip, than by hand alone (remove the hook with the fish right in the net and both in the water).

• **Creel.** A canvas creel is best. Keep it wet, and the rate of evaporation in the low-humidity Rockies will chill what's inside to near-refrigerator temperatures.

• **Fishing Vest.** You will never have enough pockets for all the fishing equipment you will end up toting about, but a fishing vest will be the closest you will come to sufficiency. I prefer the short, high "ribcage" cut vest. Longer vests always get wet around the bottom pockets when I wade deep, drowning my dry flies and my powdered fly-dry, and turning the cookies I crammed in my pocket to a gooey mess.

• **A Hat.** If you are a so-so fly caster who occasionally cracks the back of his head with an errant forward cast, you will appreciate the protection afforded by a broad-brimmed cowboy hat. Some sort of a brimmed hat is advisable in any case; the rarified air in the Rockies makes for a strong sun and bright light.

9

• **Polarized Sunglasses.** They cut the glare on the water, allow you to see rising fish more clearly, and most important, with them you can watch your step as you feel around on the bottom in chest-deep water.

• **Insect Repellent.** Generally, the Missouri's Headwater rivers are not all that buggy, but there are sufficient mosquitos to constitute an annoyance from late spring through mid-August. Small, marshy streams and high country lakes can be intolerable without repellent. Deep Woods Off seems to work the best for me.

• **Forceps.** These surgeon's tools are marvelous for removing tiny flies from a fish's mouth, and larger hooks that have been deeply ingested.

This concludes the types of tackle and equipment I commonly use on the Missouri Headwaters, with one exception. A camera. It's not exactly fishing equipment, but I promise you that you will see scenes and catch fish that you will want to remember after fishing season is over, so bring one and plenty of film.

Now, to the places where you can put all that equipment to use....

The Beaverhead

The Beaverhead River begins at Clark Canyon Dam, south of Dillon. It flows in a northeasterly direction to the town of Twin Bridges, where it joins the Big Hole to form the Jefferson. In a straight line, this translates into some fifty miles of river, but due to meanders, true river miles probably amount to sixty-five.

The Beaverhead is really two rivers if you use environment as a yardstick. From the dam to Dillon, it is a swift, well-oxygenated stream that runs down a narrow canyon, past banks choked with tall willows. Below Dillon, the river becomes slow and sluggish, with riffles, pools, meanders, and banks lined with tall cottonwoods.

The Beaverhead is like a good news/bad news joke. Of all the Missouri Headwater streams, this one rates as the sleeper. It receives little recognition, publicity, or fishing pressure, and it holds a ponderous population of trout. In fact, one stretch of river studied by a Montana Fish and Game Department shocking crew yielded a trout over four pounds *every twenty feet!* That's the good news.

Now the bad news. Of all the Missouri Headwater streams, you'll find the Beaverhead has the least access, especially if you're afoot. The fish are there, but it's hell to get to them!

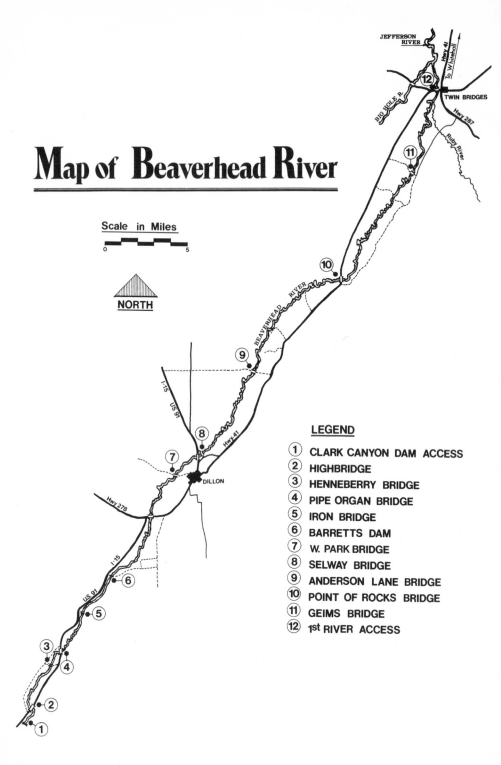

Map of Beaverhead River

Scale in Miles

0   5

NORTH

JEFFERSON RIVER

Hwy 41 To Whitehall

TWIN BRIDGES

BIG HOLE R.

Hwy 287

Ruby River

BEAVERHEAD RIVER

I-15

US 91

Hwy 41

DILLON

Hwy 278

I-15

US 91

LEGEND

① CLARK CANYON DAM ACCESS
② HIGHBRIDGE
③ HENNEBERRY BRIDGE
④ PIPE ORGAN BRIDGE
⑤ IRON BRIDGE
⑥ BARRETTS DAM
⑦ W. PARK BRIDGE
⑧ SELWAY BRIDGE
⑨ ANDERSON LANE BRIDGE
⑩ POINT OF ROCKS BRIDGE
⑪ GEIMS BRIDGE
⑫ 1st RIVER ACCESS

12

THE UPPER BEAVERHEAD, CLARK CANYON TO DILLON

The Upper Beaverhead begins at the tailrace of Clark Canyon Dam, and ends at the West Park Street Bridge, a distance of approximately 18 river miles. I-15 crosses the river six times, and the bridges are spaced between one and four miles apart. In addition, the highway right-of-way brushes by the river for a collective distance of about two miles. All in all, access above Dillon is far better than below it.

Clark Canyon Dam affords the first access. ① Take the Clark Canyon exit and turn west. A good gravel road leads down to the river on your right. The next access of consequence is Highbridge. ② Driving downriver, cross the bridge and turn left onto a gravel road. The road leads down to the river, and there is good foot and boat access there.

Near milepost 51, a gravel road leads to the river and a farm bridge (Henneberry Bridge). ③ There is virtually no foot access to the river due to bankbrush, but it's a popular float launch. You must carry a boat to the water there. Pipe Organ Bridge ④ on I-15 is a mile and a half downstream, at milepost 50, and there is foot access to the river around the bridge and from the highway below it.

Two and a half miles downstream, the highway crosses the river twice in a quarter mile. A dirt road turns left just before the first bridge and leads to an abandoned county bridge known as "Iron Bridge." ⑤ There is good foot access to the river there and a carry-boat launch.

Below Iron Bridge, there are several long stretches where the highway follows the river, and a frontage road, serving a ranch, affords access to about a quarter mile of river. Turn west at milepost 53. All access to the river on that road is before you get to the ranch.

Between milepost 54 and 55, another frontage road comes in from the east, providing some foot access for another mile downstream. The road terminates at Barretts Dam, ⑥ a large irrigation dam. There is good access for boats above the dam, and below this dam you can wade.

Below Barretts, the road leaves the river, but it crosses it once again near milepost 60, about three miles downstream. Getting to the river with a boat requires a short carry there. The next bridge is outside Dillon on a county road. ⑦ To get to it, go to the south end of Dillon's main street and take West Reeder to West Park. Follow West Park for 1½ miles. There is good foot access to the river above the bridge and irrigation dams above and below it. Both places amount to easy carries if you want to launch or retrieve a float boat.

Fishing Techniques

The Upper Beaverhead is remarkable in many ways. For one, it carries ten times the water of the river below Dillon, and it maintains bankful levels all summer long. This is because of Clark Canyon Dam, which releases a steady flow of water for downstream irrigation, a phenomenon that has several consequences. First, there is an even mix of brown and rainbow trout there. Second, the fishing holds up well all summer long, even in the middle of the day. Third, the river above Barretts Dam is unwadable, the water too swift and deep. Fourth, the tactics that take fish differ greatly from those employed downstream.

Above Barretts, the fish are almost exclusively bank oriented, due to the stable willow banks and a uniform stream bed with few fish-holding obstructions. This combination of conditions makes floating the most practical fishing method, and gives rise to a most unusual fly technique. Local anglers use a 7½-foot, 7-weight rod, with 8-weight sink-tip, weight forward line. The idea is to make short, rapid casts right into the bank; the brushier and more root-choked the water, the greater the likelihood of taking a fish. Leaders used — now get this — are in the 20-pound class, and flies are tied on 2X long-shanked stout hooks, size 2 and 4. While it would be nice to imagine trout tackle of such leviathan proportions dictated soley by the size of the fish caught, that's not entirely the case. The rule on this part of the Beaverhead is, "If you don't lose flies, you're not catching fish." You have to cast right into the root tangles to tempt these trout, and this heavy equipment is capable of wrenching loose most of the snags you'll get.

If you are fishing afoot, you will be limited to rather straight sections of stream that have been buttressed by railroad or highway riprap. This is not the fishiest water. The trout definitely prefer to station themselves around willows, but the same rule applies. Cast your fly across-current and work the bank opposite you.

Below Barretts the river calms down a bit and begins to revert to the Old Mill Stream category of environment that you'll find downstream from Dillon. More conventional fly tackle is the norm, and the river, for the most part, is wadable at normal summer levels. Caddis imitations, both adult and nymphal, are good flies to start with. Hatches of these insects are so thick on the Upper Beaverhead that they will choke you when you have the front seat in a float boat.

Spinning techniques above Barretts are identical to those employed by fly fisherman. You've got to work into the bank, and the closer you can plop a lure into the shore, the more likely you are to get a strike. Upstream casts catch more fish than downstream casts, and taking the overall swiftness of the water into consideration, you will do well to use a fast-retrieve reel. Use large, heavy lures and at least 12-pound test line, unless you have stock in a tackle company.

Below Barretts, I've had the most luck using small ¼-ounce spinners and 4-pound test line. Wade, working your lure into the current and plugging away at shadows when you're fishing in the middle of the day. Browns begin to predominate in this part of the river, and in shadow is where they'll lie.

Bait fishing is good all year long above Barretts Dam, but it is strictly a drift-fishing proposition. Sculpin have a slight edge over night-crawlers as a bait. Below Barretts, baitfishing is best after a heavy rain or during high water. There, drifted crawlers have the edge over sculpin, but there aren't many deep holes for still-fishing.

Flies
Girdle Bug
Light Spruce
Coachman Streamer
Bitch Creek
Elk Hair Caddis
Renegade

Lures
Thomas Cyclone
Panther Martin
Krocodile
Kamlooper
Hammered Silver
Fjord Spoon

THE LOWER BEAVERHEAD: DILLON TO TWIN BRIDGES

In the middle of the summer, the Lower Beaverhead rates as more of a stream than a river, due to dewatering for irrigation. But let's put semantics aside in this case and call it a river.

The environment along this stretch amounts to extensive meanders. The river enters a bend where there is usually a riffle, pours into a bank creating a deep hole, and then straightens, flattening out into a pool below. There is extensive and unusually stable bank vegetation that reaches right to the water's edge, with few bars or banks of bleached cobbles. During low water, the Beaverhead is wadable down to the mouth of the Ruby River, a fortuitous condition, as there is much posting on the river, and not all of it is of the gentlemanly "Posted, Private Land" genre that suggest you can always ask for permission to fish. Some of the signs are downright discouraging: "No Hunting — No Fishing — No Trespassing — No Nothing — And Don't Ask!"

There is also comparatively little public access to the river — five bridges in all. The Selway Bridge ⑧ lies on the northern outskirts of Dillon. Turn west on the paved county road near the Bureau of Land Management District Office and go a half mile.

The Anderson Lane Bridge ⑨ lies some seven river miles downstream. Turn west on a county gravel road near milepost 7 on Montana 41, and go 2½ miles. There is foot and boat access there.

The Point of Rocks Bridge ⑩ is at the base of Beaverhead Rock, between milepost 14 and 15, on Montana 41. It lies between nine and ten river miles below the Anderson Lane Bridge, affording foot and boat access.

The next access, Geims Bridge ⑪ is 7½ statute miles, (approximately ten river miles) downstream. Turn east on a gravel county road near milepost 22 on Highway 41. Launching a boat there requires permission from the landowner, but

17

it is regularly given.

The last access is in the town of Twin Bridges, on Highway 41. ⑫ There is a trailered boat access there, but wading access is debatable, even in mid-summer. The Beaverhead, picking up a lot of water from the Ruby River two miles above town, is swift and deep at this point.

Fishing Techniques

The Lower Beaverhead is almost exclusively a brown trout stream, which suggests several fishing tactics, whatever terminal tackle graces the end of your line. Fish into the bank, and concentrate on shadows. That's where the fish will lie. In the absence of active rising to a specific hatch, use either terrestrials (a big grasshopper is tops) or an imitation of a baitfish (a streamer, a lure, or a sculpin.) In general, the Lower Beaverhead is an afternoon/evening stream, though you'll find good fishing throughout the day if the sky is overcast. Concentrate your casting on two stations: the eddies that form up against the bank when the current boils into it at right angles; and sweepers jutting into deep pools. Sweepers are tree trunks, half in and half out of the water, that are anchored to the bank. They are swept into place during high water and almost always angle downstream, creating current discontinuities and shadows that are especially attractive to big browns.

If you are fly fishing, you will find little use for sinking line above the confluence with the Ruby River. There will be some deep holes, but you can scrape the bottom of most of them with a weighted fly. The Beaverhead runs clear due to the slow water, so if the trout turn you down, you might turn to a lighter tippet. However, start off with the heaviest leader you suspect they will accept. As soon as they realize they're hooked, Beaverhead browns tear off toward the nearest tangle of brush, and to turn them you will want the heaviest leader that is practical.

If you wish to fish aquatics, you'll probably take more but smaller fish than if you use something big and meaty on the end of your line. The most predictable hatches on the river are pale duns in the morning and caddis in the afternoon.

Should you prefer to spinfish, lean toward silver spoons that exhibit a lot of flutter and flash at slow speeds. You will also probably discover that working a lure upstream will be more productive than working it downstream. Like fly fishing, if the trout turn you down, consider going to a light-weight line. I prefer to use 6-pound test on the Beaverhead, but I always carry an extra spool loaded with 4-pound test, should I encounter foxy fish.

Baitfishing on this stretch is almost exclusively a drift fishing/sculpin proposition. Use just enough weight to sink the sculpin to the bottom, and it won't take much — a pinch or two of B-B shot. There are two exceptions to the sculpin rule: use crawlers during run-off and after the rare, heavy summer rain that clouds the water. If the grasshoppers are thick, skewer one on a #10 2X fine hook and rig it three feet below a clear plastic casting bubble. Float this rig downstream, close to the bank, and plant your feet firmly.

Whatever your fishing preferences, know that the Beaverhead has one other great bonus — the Ruby River, a major tributary. It is a fine trout stream in its own right and is often "on" when the Beaverhead is "off." Fishing techniques there

Flies
Black Maribou
  Muddler
Spuddler
Hoppers
Royal Wulff
Elk Hair Caddis
Renegade

Lures
Thomas Bouyant
Roostertail
Mepps Aglia
Wonderlure
Panther Martin
Floating Rapala

The Beaverhead River derives its name from Beaverhead Rock, named by Lewis and Clark. The rock, which strongly resembles the head of a swimming beaver when viewed from the south, was an ancient Indian landmark.

19

parallel those that work on the Beaverhead, and there is a bridge access to the river on virtually every road turning southwest off Montana 287 between Twin Bridges and Alder.

Floating

The Beaverhead above Barretts Dam is odd water to float, and I recommend you hire a guide for your first float if you're a novice (Jim Harrison, Baldy Mountain Sport Shop in Dillon, has float guides). The river is narrow and unusually swift, and the man on the oars must stay on them, or you'll be swept into a bank. Shallow riffles don't seem normal either, occurring in unexpected places, so you ground out unless you know the river well. Rafts are the best craft on this part of the river because they are maneuverable, and they slide across riffles.

There are four hazards on the river, three of them between High Bridge and Pipe Organ Bridge. Two low farm bridges are impassable at high water, and there is one sluice hole that could tip a hard-chined boat or keel canoe if you slip into it sideways. All three of these hazards come up fast. The last hazard is a series of moderate, regular waves at a place called "The Slide," about two miles below Pipe Organ Bridge. They're a piece of cake for a raft, but I suspect a jonboat or semi-vee would take some water in over the transom. You can see The Slide from the road.

Due to the swiftness of the water, float times are short. A float from High Bridge to Barretts takes 4½ hours, from Iron Bridge to Barretts, two hours. Popular put-in spots are at High Bridge, Henneberry Bridge, The Slide, and Iron Bridge. You must take out at Barretts, because of the dam.

There are vast amounts of State-owned land in Montana, but this fact alone does not necessarily mean that it is open to public trespass. When State land is leased by private concerns, they have the right to deny access. Federal lands, (BLM & Forest Service), however, are rarely closed to the public, and when they are, they are plainly posted.

Below Barretts, all the way to Twin Bridges, you will encounter two regular hazards: irrigation diversion dams and barbed wire strung across the stream to keep cattle from wandering into the wrong pasture. Most farmers have the foresight to hang flags on this wire, but bad weather often tears them down. In any case, you'll have plenty of warning. Where they occur, the Beaverhead is not swift. But as for barbed wire, I recommend that you don't float late into the evening unless you know the river well.

The float from Barretts to the West Park Bridge is best made in a raft, a jonboat, or a canoe, but you will have to carry over several fences. From Dillon to Twin Bridges, a canoe is best during low water periods. With its limited access points and sluggish pace, the Beaverhead produces long floats if you plan to be carried by the current alone. A canoe is the most practical way to hurry your pace. For example, a float from Anderson Lane Bridge to Point of Rocks Bridge takes 12 to 14 hours when the river is at its lowest stages. The float from Geims Bridge to Twin Bridges amounts to 4½ miles as the crow flies, but it takes six hours to complete.

In 1979, a devastating fish kill occurred on the Beaverhead, below Geims Bridge, when a herbicide used to clear irrigation ditches of weeds found its way into the river.

Earlier, a similar accident happened on Sixteen Mile Creek. Data from that kill indicate that a river will recover its carrying capacity in pounds in just two years! Normal age distribution — so many fingerlings, so many 12-inchers, and so many trophy-class fish — takes about four years.

The Big Hole

The Big Hole is home of a fabulous fishery set down among ideal conditions. The upper reaches of the river are cutthroat, brook trout, and grayling water — the largest natural population of these rare and beautiful fish in the lower 48 states. In the middle reaches of the river, rainbow trout predominate. In the lower river, from Glen to Twin Bridges, browns will make up the bulk of your bag. You will find whitefish everywhere in the Big Hole.

On most maps, the Big Hole begins near the town of Jackson, Montana, but you can't really call it a river at this point. It is more properly a meadow stream (see Small Streams of South-Central Montana) that twines down the middle of a lush, grassy valley, fed by countless cuts, sloughs, springs, and freshets that well up from the valley floor.

The Big Hole River derives its name from native Indians, who called valleys, "holes." Jackson Hole and the Firehole were similarly named.

In the winter, spring, and fall, the Big Hole around the town of Wisdom does approach the proportions of a river, but in the prime trout months of summer, there too it is really a meadow stream, reduced to minimal flows by irrigation dewatering.

So for our purposes, let's say the river starts below Wisdom, and that it ends at Twin Bridges, where it joins the Beaverhead to form the Jefferson, approximately 80 statute miles downstream. In river miles the distance would be more like 100 miles if you straightened out all the meanders.

If you are a fly fisherman, the Big Hole is the kind of place you would hope to find after crossing the Great Divide. Stream velocities seldom exceed the three-mile-per-hour ideal, hatches sift down like snow in the morning and evening, and the entire river conforms to a regular pattern of riffle-pool, riffle-pool. In addition, roughly half the river is within reasonable access of a road, and there are few natural barriers to wading, like impassable rapids or deep pools that surge against cliffs or brushy banks.

Although the river is so uniform in flow, gradient, and environment that it could easily be discussed as a single entity, there are a few characteristics that set sections apart. Such a division also makes access points easier to grasp on paper.

WISDOM TO WISE RIVER

This section of the river amounts to nearly 40 road miles. The Big Hole meanders extensively through private lands between Wisdom and its confluence with Pintlar Creek, 11 miles north near milepost 32. ① At that point, it straightens out, and actual river miles approximate highway miles down to Wise River.

The Big Hole/Pintlar Creek confluence also represents the place where the river becomes accessible to the highway and where the Big Hole picks up sufficient water to be called a river during the dog days of summer.

Aside from the numerous accesses afforded by

BIG HOLE

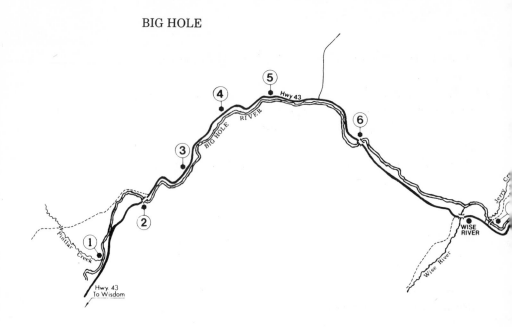

Map of the Big Hole River

Scale in Miles

NORTH

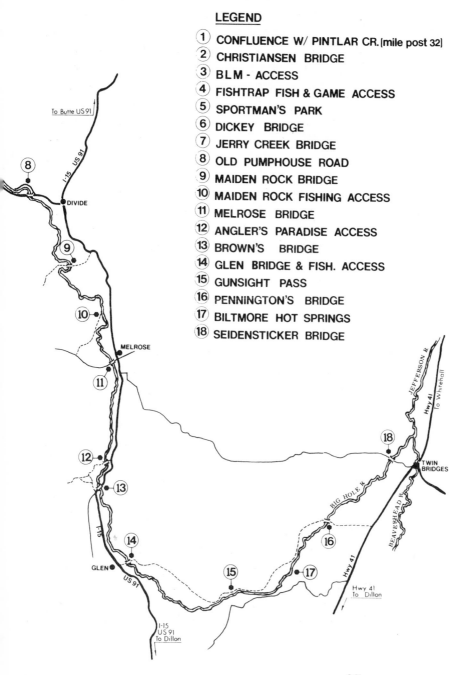

LEGEND

1. CONFLUENCE W/ PINTLAR CR. (mile post 32)
2. CHRISTIANSEN BRIDGE
3. BLM - ACCESS
4. FISHTRAP FISH & GAME ACCESS
5. SPORTMAN'S PARK
6. DICKEY BRIDGE
7. JERRY CREEK BRIDGE
8. OLD PUMPHOUSE ROAD
9. MAIDEN ROCK BRIDGE
10. MAIDEN ROCK FISHING ACCESS
11. MELROSE BRIDGE
12. ANGLER'S PARADISE ACCESS
13. BROWN'S BRIDGE
14. GLEN BRIDGE & FISH. ACCESS
15. GUNSIGHT PASS
16. PENNINGTON'S BRIDGE
17. BILTMORE HOT SPRINGS
18. SEIDENSTICKER BRIDGE

the highway right of way downstream from this point, there is public (BLM) land by the Christiansen Bridge, ② the first bridge over the river north of Wisdom. Most of this land lies downriver from the bridge, and it amounts to about a half mile of frontage on both sides of the river.

The West Big Hole Road also turns off the main highway at this point, and it's plainly marked by a sign. Although it appears to be a beckoning access road, the only place where it touches the river is in the first two miles.

Three miles downriver, near milepost 45, a dirt road turns off the main highway. It rejoins the highway at milepost 46, and affords good access to the river, on BLM land. ③ The road is a two-track, but it is impassable, because of a washout, by all except four-wheel-drive vehicles. You can get a conventional vehicle down to the water on either side of the washout.

The Fishtrap Fish and Game Access is the next public access, just below Fishtrap Creek at milepost 49. ④ Another public access, Sportman's Park, ⑤ lies three miles downstream. It's a popular place for fishermen from Butte and Anaconda, and one of the few stretches of stream still stocked with catchables by the Montana Fish and Game Department.

Dickey Bridge, ⑥ at milepost 58, marks good foot and boat access along the east bank of the river. Bryant Creek Road turns off the main highway there, and it follows the Big Hole for 2½ miles, mostly on public land. Below Dickey Bridge, the highway right of way abuts the river between milepost 62 and 63, but except for that access point, there are no public accesses before Jerry Creek Bridge, east of Wise River. To fish this stretch, you'll have to ask permission, but the ranchers on the Big Hole are uncommonly reasonable about granting it.

Fishing Techniques

Owing to the preponderance of grayling, cutts, and brookies in this stretch, you can't go wrong with a fly. It is classic water, and consequently a classic approach works best: floating lines and dry flies. You may want a little extra reach in some of the larger pools, so I suggest a weight-forward line, but other Western adaptions like shooting heads and sinking line won't be necessary. In fact, deep-sinking flies and lines are somewhat undesirable here, especially in midsummer. Because of slow flows and warm temperatures, algae grows rampant from river-bottom rocks, and any kind of terminal tackle that scrapes bottom will get clogged with goo.

In general, you'll find most of your fish in pools rather than in the riffles. Grayling and whitefish will work toward the head of the pool — sometimes even up into the lower reaches of a rifle above. Cutts, brookies, and what rainbows and browns you pick up will be toward the middle, the deepest part of the pool, and whitefish will again predominate around the pool apron. Work your fly across current or upcurrent, and except for the rare cutbank on a sharp bend, cast to the middle of the river.

Spinfishing with a lure isn't the best in this section. Riffles are really no place for a lure, and there are a lot of them. You will pick up brookies out of the pools using small spinners, but grayling and cutts are almost exclusively insect-eaters.

Flies
Royal Wulff
Coachman Wet
Hare's Ear
Muskrat Caddis
Elk Hair Caddis

Lures
Mepps Aglia
Panther Martin
Roostertail
Thomas Bouyant
Dardevle Spinnie

Then, too, when that moss grows in the summer, you'll play hell to keep a clean hook.

Baitfishing is also a practice with limited success. It's at its best in May and June, and peaks out during the salmon fly hatch, between June 1 and June 15. But at other times, flies are the effective lure, and if you can't handle the medium, you will be handicapped on the Big Hole.

Floating

During the middle of the summer, above Dickey Bridge you're a little short on water for floating, and the practice doesn't really afford all that much advantage because the river is so accessible from the road. In fact, floating on the Big Hole, except as a means of access to otherwise inaccessible pools, is not a particularly effective means of fishing. The advantage to float-fishing is that it gives you a perfect shot at the bank, but Big Hole fish are not bank-oriented. You'll get most of your strikes toward the middle of the river, and this area is usually best fished from shore. The river is really a wader's dream, with one exception — during the salmon fly hatch, but there is a good reason. The hatch coincides with high water, high enough to create stations along the bank. Salmon flies nearly always enter the water along the bank, so at this time trout pile up there.

Below Dickey Bridge, floating is more practical. The river winds through private lands, and the riffles will have enough water to skid you over the rocks. A raft is my choice on the Big Hole for that reason; rafts slide over, rather than collide with rocks, and there are a lot of them in the riffles.

The first downriver access below Dickey Bridge will be approximately 3½ river miles away, where the Big Hole brushes the highway. You will have to carry the boat up or down a steep embankment. The next access is the Jerry Creek Bridge, ⑦ a mile east of Wise River and approximately 4½ river miles downstream. Turn north onto the first gravel road after you leave town. You can see the bridge from the highway, and you can get a trailer down to the water there.

WISE RIVER TO GLEN

Although I resist making such judgments, I must call this stretch my personal favorite — not because it has more or larger fish, but because it is my idea of perfect trout water: a captivating blend of gentle hydraulics, pools, shade trees, pastures, boulders, and even a canyon thrown in for good measure.

There is good (nearly unlimited) access to the river via Highway 43 for seven miles downstream from the Jerry Creek Bridge. The Old Pumphouse Road ⑧ leaves the highway between milepost 73 and 74 and rejoins it at milepost 75, by the Divide Bridge. There is some foot access to the river along this road.

The highway leaves the river for some 10 miles after the Divide Bridge, rejoining it near the town of Melrose. There is access to the river at Maiden Rock Bridge ⑨ (turn right at milepost 101 off the Frontage Road) and across the railroad tracks between milepost 96 and 97. There are also two miles of access on the opposite side of the river — the Maiden Rock Fishing Access. ⑩ To get there, you must go to Melrose and cross the Big Hole (there will be two bridges). Bear right for six miles

Lewis and Clark were the first white men to see the Big Hole. They originally named it the Wisdom River, the name source of the towns of Wise River and Wisdom.

29

on a county road. If you have conventional wheels or a large RV, don't go beyond the first campground. The road continues for about a mile and a half, but the first hill is rough, rocky, and steep, and the road beyond gradually disintegrates into a jeep trail. There is beautiful fly water all along the access.

A word of warning: don't confuse the Maiden Rock Bridge with the Maiden Rock Access. They are two different places, and the confusion is fueled further by the signs that identify each place. You get to the Access via Melrose, and to the bridge by turning off the old highway at milepost 101. In this case, you might say that you shouldn't take any Rock for granite.

The Melrose Bridge ⑪ is the next access downstream. Angler's Paradise Bridge, ⑫ just below milepost 89, is next, coming up fast, tree and brush-shaded; it is difficult to see from the highway, so look sharp.

Between Angler's Paradise Bridge and Brown's Bridge, ⑬ two miles downstream, there is foot access to the river over the railroad tracks. There is some pretty fly water there, and classic worm holes around the abutments of Brown's Bridge and the railroad bridge just upstream.

The river wanders away from the road after Brown's Bridge, and the next drive-up access is at the Glen Bridge and Fishing Access ⑭ , four miles downstream.

Along these four miles, there are three walk-in accesses. These amount to permissable corridors of trespass, provided by a generous rancher. You may walk to the river without obtaining permission. These places are posted as such and easily seen from Highway 41. Treat this opportunity with special attention to landowner rights and go out of your way to prove that sportsmen and gentlemen are the same people.

Fishing Techniques

This stretch of the Big Hole is a gentleman's stream, with the trout that live there keeping respectable hours. In summer, fishing is best from sunrise until eleven or twelve o'clock. Action resumes around four and continues until dusk. On cloudy days, fish will feed right through mid-day.

Dries are the most effective — and the most fun — at this time. You can't go wrong with some sort of caddis imitation, and in late July and early August, big spruce moths flutter about and tumble into the water, luring large trout up to the top.

The best way to zero in on these feeding fish is a simple matter of stream watching. Draw up a rock at the head of a pool and watch for rises upstream and down. Generally, you'll find the most activity from the riffle at the head of a pool to its middle reaches. A lot of the slapping and slurping, flipping and flopping will be whitefish, but you can keep most of them off your hook by using #14 or larger flies. Personally, I get a kick out of catching whitefish and would much rather catch ten whitefish and five trout than five trout.

In quieter pools, you will probably be looking at brown trout. In the bubbly riffle at a pool's head and in the pockets that form behind emerged boulders in the canyon areas, the odds say you'll come up with a rainbow. When the spruce moths are fluttering, look for rises along the bank.

When trout turn down caddis patterns, try a #16 or #18 imitation of a pale dun, or a small Light Cahill on a fine tippet — 5X or 6X. I have found that one of these two approaches will take fish every time.

In the fall and spring, before high water, the Big Hole is ripe for streamers. Streamers are also the route to take when trout turn off in the middle of hot, summer days. Another point to remember when you are confronted with turned-off trout is that the Big Hole is a caddis and stonefly stream, with comparatively few mayflies, so concentrate on patterns that imitate the critters most in demand.

The Big Hole also has a memorable salmon fly hatch, reputed to be the most prolific of all the Missouri Headwater streams. If you hanker to take a trophy trout on a fly, late May to the end of June is the time when you stand your best chance. If the hatch has not yet emerged, fish large stonefly nymphs right on the bottom. If the flies are on the bankbrush, use an imitation of an adult, but fish it wet. You will take twice the trout under the surface than you will hook on top.

Flies
Henryville
Goddard Caddis
Potts Flies
Royal Wulff
Wright's Royal

Except for the period preceding the salmon fly hatch, you will be well and fully served by a floating line throughout the angling year. Although there are deep pools in this part of the river, if you pick your path carefully, you can wade within casting distance of any station in the stream.

Lures
Panther Martin
Mepps Aglia
Pearl Dardevle
Hammered Silver
Hammered Brass

Spinfishing with a lure is most productive in the early spring, and through the fall, when the water is at normal levels. If you're stuck with a spinning rod when the water is low, fish the deeper pools very early and very late, or in the middle of the day, when the fish are not rising to flies. In the middle of the day, hug the bottom with your retrieve, where the fish will lie because there are cooler temperatures and more oxygen there.

Another point to consider when the Big Hole is dewatered is very light line — 3- or 4-pound test — and when the fish turn down large lures, go to very small lures, ¼- to ⅜-ounce. Start off with silver in midsummer, and use copper or brass when the water is up.

If there is a large insect hatch on the water, with trout slapping all around, prepare yourself for frustration if you insist on fishing with lures alone. In this case, you'd be well advised to try a plastic casting bubble and a fly. More so than in any other river in the Missouri Headwaters, trout in the Big Hole just aren't interested in jewelry when they are zeroing in on flies.

Baitfishing, like lure fishing, is only marginally successful from mid-July to the first frost. Before and after that time, drift-fishing a sculpin through the heads of holes is the approach that appeals to most fish. Baitfishing is also deadly during the salmon fly hatch. Sink an adult with a pinch of B-B shot and drift it along deep banks.

Owing to the prolific and sometimes hermongus hatches of insects along the Big Hole, you may be able to use a real fly as a bait at times other than at the salmon fly hatch. If trout are popping at insects roughly a half-inch or larger, put one on a #16 2X Fine hook. Fish it three feet below a clear plastic casting bubble and drift it down with the current, manipulating the drift in such a way that the fly stays well away from the bubble. Don't watch the fly though — watch the bubble. When it makes the slightest bob, strike. When conditions make this trick possible (many insects that hatch out are too small to hook), it is unbelievably effective.

Floating

As is the case above Wise River, in this part of the Big Hole, look upon a float boat as transportation from pool to pool, rather than as a fishing craft. You will find the most fish in the middle of the river.

Another rule of thumb is that you'll make about one river mile per hour when you stop to fish the more attractive holes, so plan your trip accordingly.

There is trailered boat access at the Jerry Creek Bridge and at the Pumphouse Bridge, above the Pumphouse Dam. You must pull out at this point, as the dam is not navigable.

A mile and a half downstream, there is a trailer launch at Divide Bridge. The next trailer take-out is at the Melrose Bridge, 10 miles downstream, and 5 miles below it, at Angler's Paradise Bridge, there is another ramp. Between Angler's Paradise and Brown's Bridge, there is a diversion dam that you must carry around and debatable trailer access to the water (you'll probably need a four-by) at the Glen Access. All other access points require that you carry your boat to the water.

The floating from Jerry Creek Bridge to Melrose is generally through canyon country, with a lot of emerged boulders to navigate around. Below Melrose, the river gentles out and deepens, and as you approach Glen, snag-trees begin to become a nuisance. All in all, the floating is easy, with plenty of time to prepare for whatever hazards you will encounter.

GLEN TO TWIN BRIDGES

The Big Hole from the Glen Access to Twin Bridges represents approximately 24 river miles. Getting to the river along this stretch requires more effort than to the river above, because it is served by gravel and dirt roads that are at times in poor condition.

The best access to the river is via the Burma Road, which turns off Highway 43 at the Glen Fishing Access and connects with Highway 41 south of Twin Bridges, at milepost 23, a total of 18 road miles. During dry weather, I wouldn't hesitate to take a car down the Burma Road. When it's wet, I'd want a four-wheel-drive. After a wet period, the road will be rutted and bouncy.

Most of the road is a wide county road, a little short on gravel. From the Reichle Ranch to Gunsight Pass, ⑮ the road becomes a narrow two-track that winds well above the river and in places is carved into a cliff. Due to the rocky roadbed, it's passable even under wet conditions, but take care as you round curves. There's a surprising volume of traffic on the road.

Montana law requires that you ask permission to trespass on private property whether the land is posted or not.

Access afforded by this road is along the two-track section, about three miles of river frontage. You have to walk down to the river along this route, with the exception of one point on the upstream side of Gunsight Pass. Another access lies at Pennington's Bridge, ⑯ near Twin Bridges.

The Biltmore Road affords one access to the other side of the river. It turns off I-15 at Apex and joins up with Highway 41 between Dillon and Twin Bridges at milepost 20. There's a private access at the Biltmore Hot Springs, ⑰ a locally popular swimming hole.

Seidensticker Bridge, ⑱ west of Twin Bridges, is the last access point on the Big Hole. Take Montana 361 south of town and drive for 1½ miles. If you follow this road, it will take you over to Melrose. It is a well-maintained, all-weather gravel road that cuts considerable mileage off the Dillon route, but it affords no access to the Big Hole.

Because of the effort and adventure associated with getting to this portion of the river, it receives relatively light pressure. There is excellent fly and lure water from the Reichle Ranch to Gunsight Pass, and fly, lure, and bait water around Pennington's Bridge (there are two bridges there). Seidensticker Bridge is riffly water, but there are pools that you can wade to up and downstream.

This stretch of the Big Hole is characterized by extensive meandering and braiding of the river bed. There are frequent snags in the river, plus an unusual hazard: when gusty winds kick up, take a good look at any nearby trees. Due to an unusually high beaver population, there are a lot of half-chewed cottonwoods along the bank, and they come down during high winds with enough regularity to warrant some caution.

FISHING TECHNIQUES

The population pendulum swings toward brown trout between Glen and Twin Bridges, suggesting some subtle changes in stations and approach. Here I've had the most luck fishing into brushy banks and around the many snags lodged in the river bed.

Your selection of terminal tackle should also be in time with the beat of a different drum. There are good hatches in the morning and afternoon, but you'll catch larger trout if you'll use streamers, bucktails, or big stonefly nymphs. If you're after these larger fish, get up early, siesta during the middle of the day, and fish late, until dark. You will take trout in the middle of the day, but they will be the small foolish ones. You will also find excellent angling for trophy browns in the spring, before high water, and in the fall, after the first frost. Summer irrigation water is returned to the river below Glen, but it has the effect of warming the water to a point where the trout go sullen. If you are fishing in mid-summer, the early morning hours are the best of all, when the water is coolest.

You will find a sink-tip line useful along this stretch. There are many deep holes, and if you're after browns, it's sometimes necessary to get to the very bottom of the river. Another tactic to investigate is night fishing. Use a large light-colored fly and fish it dry. At times it pays to work these flies so they create a surface disturbance.

The predominance of browns leads me to conclude that this is the kindest stretch of the Big Hole to the lure fisheman. The same basics hold true as those that guide the fly man: fish early, late, and toward brush piles and the bank. I have had success on large gold spinners in the spring, small silver spinners in the summer, and gold spoons, with fluorescent dots or stripes, in the fall.

Baitfishing brings the best results if you drift-fish a sculpin along the banks and brushpiles, but in all honesty, except for during the salmon fly hatch, there are better rivers in the area for natural baits. The Big Hole just doesn't have the dramatic changes in bottom or bank structure that lend themselves to traditional bait techniques.

Flies
Black Maribou
    Muddler
Yellow Maribou
    Muddler
Matuka Muddler
Spuddler
Spruce

Lures
Krocodile
Kamlooper
Wonderlure
Thomas Cyclone
Panther Martin

37

FLOATING

Float-fishing becomes a more workable approach from Glen to Twin Bridges because browns are bank-oriented fish. Some oarwork will be in order due to frequent snags, but aside from them, and from the possibility of blow-downs from beaver chews during high winds, there are no special hazards save for the occasional and avoidable irrigation diversion dams.

Favorite put-in and take-out spots are at the Glen Access, at Gunsight Pass on the Burma Road, at the Biltmore Hot Springs, and at Seidensticker Bridge. There is a short carry to the water at Pennington's Bridge, and a modest launch fee is charged at the Biltmore Hot Springs.

It is approximately 5½ miles from Glen to Gunsight Pass, 3 miles from Gunsight Pass to the Biltmore Hot Springs, 5 miles from the Hot Springs to Pennington's Bridge, and 5 miles from Pennington's Bridge to Seidensticker Bridge. Figure your progress at about a mile an hour.

If you are floating this part of the river for the first time, always take the channel that is moving the most water. Several side channels split again before re-entering the river, and you will ground out on their shallow bars.

The Gallatin

The headwaters of the Gallatin lie within Yellowstone National Park, and the river ends at the Three Forks of the Missouri, approximately 100 miles downstream. As it follows its course, the river rushes through the Gallatin Canyon; then it meanders through the Gallatin Valley. The mouth of the Gallatin Canyon, 6 miles above the town of Gallatin Gateway, marks the midpoint of the river, and its transition from relatively fast to relatively slow water. Above the canyon, the river is called the Upper Gallatin. Below this point it's known as the Lower Gallatin.

With the exception of a small stretch of stream in the Park, the Upper Gallatin has free access from U.S. Highway 191. Most of the river is within looking distance of the road, and the remotest pool is no further than a five minute walk from your car.

In contrast, the Lower Gallatin is bordered almost exclusively by private lands, and in places it wanders nearly two miles from the nearest road. Public access points are spotty, but though there is substantial posting of private lands, permission to fish is usually easy to come by. Passing the time of day with a landowner often opens up private access points too. Virtually every ranch along the Gallatin has a dirt road that leads down to the river.

The Gallatin River was named by Lewis and Clark to honor Albert Gallatin, Secretary of the Treasury under Presidents Jefferson and Madison.

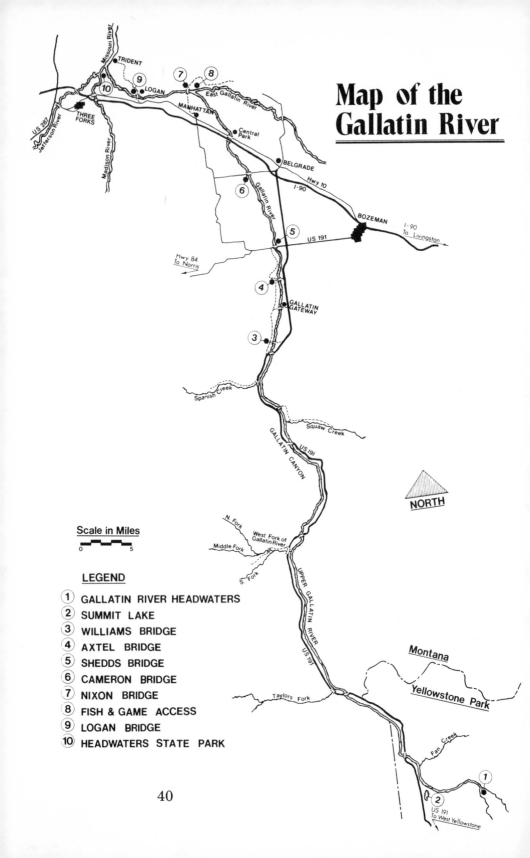

Map of the Gallatin River

TRIDENT

Missouri River

LOGAN

THREE FORKS

US 287

Jefferson River

Madison River

MANHATTAN

East Gallatin River

Central Park

BELGRADE

Hwy 10

I-90

Gallatin River

BOZEMAN

I-90
To Livingston

US 191

Hwy 84
To Norris

GALLATIN GATEWAY

Spanish Creek

Squaw Creek

GALLATIN CANYON

US 191

NORTH

Scale in Miles
0   5

LEGEND
① GALLATIN RIVER HEADWATERS
② SUMMIT LAKE
③ WILLIAMS BRIDGE
④ AXTEL BRIDGE
⑤ SHEDDS BRIDGE
⑥ CAMERON BRIDGE
⑦ NIXON BRIDGE
⑧ FISH & GAME ACCESS
⑨ LOGAN BRIDGE
⑩ HEADWATERS STATE PARK

N. Fork

West Fork of Gallatin River

Middle Fork

S. Fork

UPPER GALLATIN RIVER

US 191

Montana

Yellowstone Park

Taylors Fork

Fan Creek

US 191
To West Yellowstone

40

The Gallatin offers easy fishing from a technical point of view. With far more regularity than the Madison, Yellowstone, or Missouri, the river conforms to the riffle-pool, riffle-pool scheme of streamflow most of us have come to know. Hence, it is easier to read and to interpret.

It is also more intimate than any of its sister streams, with thickly-forested banks, a cool, green atmosphere, and a volume of flow you can cope with.

The trout species in the Gallatin include cutthroat, cutthroat/rainbow cross-breeds, rainbow trout, brown trout, and brookies. Cutthroat are found at the river's headwaters, rainbows predominate in the Gallatin Canyon, and browns are in the majority along the Lower Gallatin. Brookies are spotty throughout the river, usually concentrated around the mouths of small tributaries, and at irrigation headgates.

Because the Gallatin flows wild and is unencumbered by dams, it is subject to extreme high water conditions during spring run-off, a stage that commonly lasts from the third week of May until the last week of June. Contrary to popular belief, fishing is excellent during high water, but it is strictly a bait proposition.

Once this flood stage passes its highest point, the river begins to clear, and the change often occurs overnight. It signals the time when lures will be most appealing to trout, a period that lasts about three weeks. The river reaches normal summer levels and total clarity between the second and third week of July, and from that time until the snow flies, the Gallatin is ripe for flies.

THE GALLATIN IN THE PARK

The Gallatin begins as a series of springs, freshets, and alpine lakes that lie between two and three miles east of U.S. 191, near Summit Lake ①, ②.

Above its confluence with Fan Creek, the Gallatin rates as a small stream rather than a river, but soon after it joins Fan Creek, it picks up enough water to swell its bed to an average width of 75 feet.

The character of the river in the Park makes it ideal for fly fishing. The pitch of the bed is gentle, and the river meanders extensively. The banks are stable, lined with grasses and low willow, making for easy casting. Deep cut banks lie on the outside of bends. These are the most likely lies for trout in this section of the river, followed by pools that form at the base of riffles.

In the absence of actively-rising fish, the most consistently productive technique here is to quarter a cast down-current that will carry a weighted nymph into a deep hole. If you are addicted to dry fly fishing, try working a terrestrial into the bank. The vegetation is home to an unusually large number of grasshoppers, ants, beetles, and other creepy-crawlies; and with a terrestrial imitation, you can often coax a rise from trout that are feeding below the surface.

This part of the Gallatin is also superb fly fishing during the salmon fly hatch. The hatch reaches the river's upper limits around the last week of June, and although the river will be high, it always remains relatively clear down to its confluence with Taylor's Fork. This is not true downstream of this point. When the hatch is on, the river below Taylor's Fork runs chocolate with mud, and baitfishing with live nymphs or salmon flies is the only practical way to fish.

Spinning with lures is a technique that takes a back seat to fly fishing in the Park. Rainbows and cutthroat predominate, and in their typical 10- to 14-inch sizes, they have a decided preference for an insect diet. If you prefer to spin, you will get the most strikes if you use equipment suited to four-pound test line, and quarter ounce gold or silver spinners. Fish them as you would a fly, quarter-casting downcurrent, and into the deeper holes and cutbanks.

Flies
Montana Nymph
Muskrat Caddis
Sandy Mite
Hoppers
Irresistable

Lures
Panther Martin
Mepps Aglia
Roostertail
Little Jewel
Thomas Cyclone

TAYLOR'S FORK TO WEST FORK

The Gallatin drops more rapidly below Taylor's Fork, changing the character of the river as well as your fishing approach. Here the river is studded with emerged boulders, and it is shallow and swift.

The most common stations occur in the slow pockets of water that form behind boulders, and the easiest way to fish them with a lure or a fly is by casting upcurrent. Place your cast so it falls along the eddy fence that forms on either side of the calm pocket, or into the still pool directly behind the rock. Three casts should be enough to test the water; if you get no results, move on. When working this stretch, the angler who covers the most water will catch the most fish.

Working the back side of boulders is especially well-suited to dry fly fishing. Use a light colored, high floating dry tied on a #12 or #14 hook. This is fast water, and large, bright patterns are the easiest to follow.

The second most common station will be in deep

The broad valley between the mouth of Porcupine Creek and the West Fork is the winter range for the Gallatin Elk herd.

Hundreds of these animals can often be seen from the road during the months of February and March.

channels in the river bed. If you are good at reading water, you will be able to identify those channels by the surface appearance of the slower, calmer water that rides above them. When the sun is on the river is the easiest time to find the channels; the river rocks will be bright tan to gray in the shallows, but they will have a greenish tint in the channels.

Channels commonly take the form of an extended oval, and trout feed toward the front of the upstream end of the oval. They receive food as it is swept down to them from the shallows above, and the best presentation is a cast quartered across current, then drifted down to the waiting fish.

The third most common station along this stretch of the Gallatin lies in bank eddies — slow swirls of deep water caused by the braking effect of highway riprap or an abrupt bend in the river. These are best worked from the river into the bank, and with a cast that drifts your fly or lure from shallows to the hole.

Bait fishing is not the best in the Gallatin above West Fork, and it's largely because the river lacks deep holes there. You'll always find the best bait fishing for trout in slow, sullen pools and eddies where you can't see the bottom, and there's little of that kind of water in this stretch. Like all rules of thumb, however, this one has an exception: when you are in the middle of the salmon fly hatch. A pinch of b-b split shot six inches above a live salmon fly skewered on a #8 hook is the best rigging. Fish the bait wet and close in to the bank, and you'll do well.

If you're a fly fisherman, one peculiarity of this stretch is worthy of note. Because of its unstable soil, the Taylor Fork drainage will run muddy and cloud the Gallatin after no more than a modest rain. But once you get above Taylor Fork, you'll find water clear enough for flies all season long, except at flood stage.

WEST FORK TO THE CANYON MOUTH

At West Fork, the Gallatin enters a twisting canyon of rock parapets, white water and mountain peaks that scrape the sky. Although the gradient of the river is steep all the way to the canyon mouth, there is more variety of water here than above: swift rapids, champagne riffles, and deep, green pools.

The trick to fishing this stretch of the Gallatin lies in matching your tackle to stream conditions. For practical purposes, standard fly fishing gear isn't suited to working either swift or deep water so if you're tickled with feathers, look instead to the shallow tail end of pools and to attractive-looking water where you can make out the bottom. As a rule, the best water for working a fly will be found immediately above big rapids.

Covering the small pools behind emerged boulders is another good bet. The machinery of a river piles sediment there, and even of these pockets are bordered by bottomless holes, the trout that fin there will be within sight range of a dry fly.

If there are no actively-rising trout, start fishing with a streamer or a large nymph. Because of the power and depth of the river, you'll probably be limited to cross-current or down current casts. This is one place where it would be wise to pack your reel arbor with a Hi-D sinking tip.

West Fork also marks the beginning of that section of the Gallatin that is best-suited to spin and bait fishing. From West Fork downstream to the Three Forks, you'll find broad, deep channels and large rotating eddies on every bend in the river.

The overall power of the Gallatin down to the canyon mouth dictates comparatively heavy terminal tackle when you're spinning with lures. It is not purely a matter of weight, either. In order to get down to the fish, you need a lure with a small profile in relation to its total weight. Put another way, a half ounce lure the size of your fist would ride a lot higher than a half ounce lure the size of your thumbnail. It is this latter class of hardware that usually catches the most trout in swift, deep water.

The most productive casting techniques are usually either a cross-current cast at a pool head, or a retrieve up an eddy fence. To execute the former, lob your lure across the swift water funneling into a pool, and let the current carry it in a broad, looping arc. Reel slowly — or not at all — until your line points almost directly downstream. This technique will have your lure nearly bouncing bottom, where the trout will station in a pool.

An eddy fence is the confused current line that divides fast and slow water. Fences form downstream of any stationary object in the river. Trout lie in the calm water to pick off food drifting by in the fast water, so if you place your cast so your retrieve plots the vague line the fence defines, your lure will pass in front of any trout there. You can work an eddy fence upcurrent or downcurrent, with equal effect.

Baitfishing along this stretch of the Gallatin is usually a nightcrawler and splitshot proposition, unless you are in the middle of the salmon fly hatch. The key to success is to keep your bait moving. Two places will be best: deep, swirling pools next to the bank; and slow-moving channels in midstream where you can't see bottom.

When fishing the bank holes, you will have to work the bait. Slowly draw it across the bottom by gently raising your rod tip; then reel down to the water to take up the slack you've gained. This approach allows the sensitive rod tip to telegraph a bite. Bites are hard to feel if you work a bait directly off a reel.

Midstream channels are best fished by drift fishing. Weight your bait so that it occasionally ticks bottom, but doesn't hang up. Quarter a cast upstream and drift the worm down through the channel until you no longer feel the bounce of bottom. If you are correctly weighted, you will be quartered downstream when the bouncing stops.

Drift fishing is a highly effective technique in all the rivers and streams in the area, but it is not an easy art to master. What is most difficult about it is learning the difference between the feel of bouncing bottom and the rap-rap-rap of a trout tugging at your line. Florescent, easy-to-see line is the key to telling the difference. As your bait is drifting along, keep a sharp eye on the place where your line enters the water. If the line is moving along with the current, the tick you feel is the rap of riverbed rocks. If it is stationary, with the river rushing on by it, and you still feel "bottom," there's a trout down there gnawing away at your bait.

CANYON MOUTH TO CAMERON BRIDGE

On this stretch of water, the Gallatin slows down and catches its breath. The river meanders through rich bottomlands and often breaks up into several side channels, each a separate trout stream in its own right.

This phenomenon, known as "braiding," tends to increase the available food supply for trout. It's an educated guess, but there are probably more trout per acre foot of water between the canyon mouth ③ and Cameron Bridge ⑥ than in any other section of the Gallatin.

This is also an excellent place to visit if you like to fish more intimate water than is typical of our booming Western rivers. The side streams range from 10 to 40 feet in width, and all of them incorporate the same riffle/pool structure that is common above.

Access is something of a problem; there are only five points where the river is readily accessible, and they are all bridges. There's a bright side to this situation, however; the lack of easy access limits the fishing pressure. If you expend the time and energy to get there, you probably will have the river to yourself.

If you are a spin fisherman, you'll probably find the stream conditions most to your liking upstream of Shedd's Bridge ⑤, on Highway 189. If you are a fly fisherman, prospect downstream from there. This is not to say that trout won't take a fly around the canyon mouth, or a spinner by Cameron Bridge — only that the Gallatin slows its pace the more downstream you go, and as a rule, fly fishing is most productive in flat water.

When you fish with a fly, you'll be able to match

most of the conditions you'll encounter with a floating line. You'll catch the most fish using nymphs, the largest fish, using streamers. If trout are rising to a hatch, and you can't match it, try using a Light Cahill, an Elk Hair Caddis, or a Ginger or Cream Bivisible. These patterns always seem to have appeal on the Gallatin, because they resemble the caddis (locally known as "willow flies") that are forever buzzing among the bank willows. In August, you can't go wrong by working a grasshopper imitation into the bank from early afternoon until sundown.

If you prefer to spin with lures, the principal to remember is to use a small spinner when the water is brilliantly clear and large (up to ⅝ oz.) spoons when the water is cloudy. Quarter your casts upcurrent and direct your retrieve through places where you can't see bottom.

Spinning with bait is productive on this stretch during high water, and it is also good later on, if you'll fish after a rain or a heavy shower. This is especially true when it rains in the evening or during the night. The moisture brings worms up to the surface, and many of them tumble into the water. By first light, every trout in the river is primed for a meat diet.

Getting back to the matter of access, although floating may seem like an ideal way to get around the problem, it isn't. This part of the river is loaded with floating hazards: log jams that reach clear across the channel, shallow bars that must be portaged, and makeshift diversion dams for irrigation water. It can be floated, but it is neither a pleasant float nor a safe one.

Flies
Royal Wulff
Goofus Bug
Montana Nymph
Muddler
Wooly Worm

Lures
Panther Martin
Hammered Silver
Pearl Dardevle
Mepps
Thomas Cyclone

CAMERON BRIDGE TO
THE EAST GALLATIN

This part of the river rates as an oddity. It is subjected to extensive dewatering in late July and August, when farmers divert the river to irrigate fields. The limited amount of free-flowing water in turn reduces the total trout population. On a trout-per-gallons-of-water basis, this stretch of the Gallatin has the fewest fish when the river is at normal stages.

However, when the river is at its lowest levels, what resident trout do exist, crowd into deep, dark holes, building up more than substantial concentrations of fish. In short, you can find some great fishing there when the river bed looks bleached white and dry as a bone.

Don't expect that good fishing will come easy, though. The water will be so clear that you'll be able to see the bottom in ten-foot deep holes. And even though the trout are not unduly pressured here, they are spooky because they are so vulnerable.

This is the place to wear neutral-colored clothing and to carefully stalk your fish. Use artificials and a light touch when casting; and spiderweb lines and long leaders. In the same vein, #16 to #22 nymphs and dries, and thumbtack-sized ultra lite lures will fetch you the most strikes. And always come into your fish from the back side.

There will be many shallow, pond-like pools that won't hold trout. Pass them by and concentrate on black pools that are fed by live water. The volume of flow entering these places doesn't seem to be important. You will find as many trout below a trickle as you will below a good-sized stream.

Another peculiarity of this area is that the diverted water from the Gallatin commonly ends up in live stream beds — meandering spring creeks that are the result of the cutting and draining of boggy marshes by settlers a hundred years ago. The rich bottomlands of the Gallatin between Belgrade and Manhattan are laced with these creeks, some of them substantial streams, and they support rich populations of trout that can be taken with flies, lures, or bait.

As is the case with nearly all of the Lower Gallatin, fishing in the river and in the creeks it spawns is on private land. Although farmers in the area are noted for their old-time hospitality, be forewarned that many of them do not allow fishing on Sunday because of religious convictions.

THE EAST GALLATIN TO
THE THREE FORKS

By the time the Gallatin reaches the mouth of the East Gallatin, it has picked up a good deal of the water that was diverted above. The additional volume contributed to the Gallatin makes it more a river than a stream. This is big water, on a par with the Madison and Jefferson.

There are four public accesses to this stretch: a fish and game access north of Manhattan⑧; the Nixon Bridge⑦; the Logan Bridge, west of Logan⑨; and the Headwaters State Park, south of Trident. ⑩. There is good foot access throughout the State Park and west of the Logan Bridge. Cross the bridge and walk west along the railroad tracks. The tracks border the river in a dozen places between the bridge and the Three Forks.

During the heyday of rail travel, palatial stations were built in tiny towns to serve the tourists who came to Yellowstone Park. The Northern Pacific, Milwaukee, Union Pacific, and Great Northern Railroads were all represented.

The huge station in Logan, Montana, has since been torn down, but these remnants of a bygone era remain in West Yellowstone, Gallatin Gateway and Livingston.

If you enjoy float fishing, this stretch rates as an excellent bet. There is sufficient water all year round to float a boat, and the conditions you'll encounter rate between novice and sub-intermediate on the white water scale. The float from Manhattan to Logan is the easiest. Logan to the Three Forks gets a little tricky because of occasional log jams and extensive braiding of the river. Both floats take about an hour and a half, if you drift straight through. When you stop to test attractive-looking water, each stretch will take a half day.

Whether you're floating or fishing from the bank, you'll do best by using big-water tackle and techniques. You'll probably use sink-tip line most of the time. Use big flies too: #4 to #6 streamers, and #6 to #10 nymphs. Hatches tend to come off this stretch of the Gallatin early — between first light and an hour after sun-up — and between two and four in the afternoon, if you prefer to fish dry. As a rule, trout on the rise here aren't too con-concerned about fly size — use a #14 or #12 — but they can be selective about colors, so carry a good assortment of dries.

When spinning with lures, you should think big too. Pack spoons and spinners in the ⅜ to ⅝-ounce class. Because the East Gallatin flows through intensively farmed lands, it carrys a heavy silt load, making this stretch of the Gallatin milky, even in August. The cloudy water eliminates the need for ultra-light lines, so you can use 6- or 8-pound test here. Another tip: carry a few lures with a dash of florescent red. I can't say why, but it is a highly attractive color to trout when the water is less than crystal clear.

Because of this same milkiness, baitfishing is

productive on this last part of the Gallatin all year long. This is one place I recommend you go if you, your wife, or the kids are not accomplished in the finer points of fly, lure, or bait fishing. Just find a deep, swirling hole (and there are plenty of them), rig up with a sinker and a #6 snelled baitholder hook, and bait it with a nitecrawler or a strip of sucker meat. Cast the bait up toward the head of the hole, cradle your rod in a forked stick and settle back to wait. Hundreds of trophy-class trout and thousands of trout dinners have been caught here by using just this technique.

The Jefferson

The Jefferson River begins at the confluence of the Big Hole and Beaverhead Rivers, one mile north of the town of Twin Bridges. It flows in a northerly direction for approximately 50 miles and ends at the Three Forks, where it joins the Madison and Gallatin Rivers to form the Missouri.

In its entirety, the Jefferson rates as slow water by comparison with other Headwater streams. Bed structure is characterized by typically long, quiet pools connected by short, shallow riffles. This nature translates further into stable, well-vegetated banks, without the bone-white and bleached stretches of cobbles, pebbles, and bars common to swifter rivers. The ambience of the Jeff is that of the old swimming hole: a gentle, reflective place to fish, where flies buzz on warm summer afternoons.

These conditions do lead to one negative feature of the river — there are huge populations of trash fish: carp, chubs, suckers, and whitefish. However, the same web of natural order that gives rise to these undesirables has a positive side. The Jefferson amounts to a perfect environment for brown trout — big brown trout — and it also rates as the least-fished river in the Missouri Headwaters.

For purposes of discussion, it's best to divide the Jefferson into three parts: from Twin Bridges to the Cardwell Fishing Access; the Jefferson River Canyon; and Sappington Bridge to the Three Forks.

TWIN BRIDGES TO CARDWELL

The Jefferson begins a mile north of Twin Bridges. Virtually all the land bordering the river is private, so access amounts to one of several choices along this stretch: obtain permission to trespass; or float; or wade below the mean high water mark, upriver or down, from one of the bridge crossings or Fish and Game Access sites along the river.

The first river access is right in the middle of Twin Bridges, on the Beaverhead River. ① Because of the character of the Beaverhead at this point, wading down to the Jeff is a chancy proposition at any time except at extreme low water. It's also a long walk — about 1½ river miles. This is primarily a float access. Turn toward Dillon on Montana 41; you can park a car and get to the river on the south side of the bridge. There's no launching ramp for a trailered boat, but you can get right next to the bank. I can't imagine any float craft, from a canoe to a McKenzie, that couldn't be dropped into the water at this point.

The next access is six miles north along Montana 41. ② It is an irrigation diversion dam, on a large side-channel of the river that touches the shoulder of the highway. You can see it from the road. Like the Twin Bridges Access, there is no launching ramp, but with a little muscle power, you can get a heavy boat on a trailer. An aluminum car-topper or a raft are easy to take out here.

Foot access is possible at this point, in all but high water stages of the river. Wade upstream. The main channel is a half mile away. There are also good foot access and boat take-out points on the west side of the river, beginning approximately

Map of Jefferson River

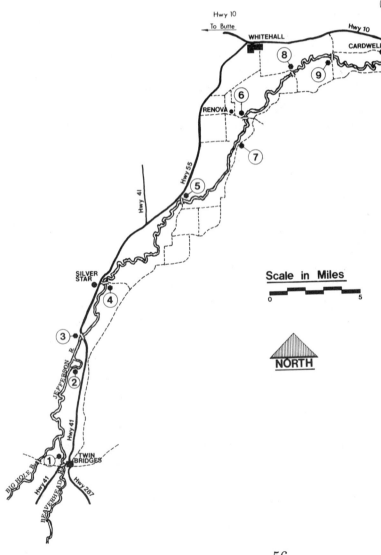

Scale in Miles

0   5

NORTH

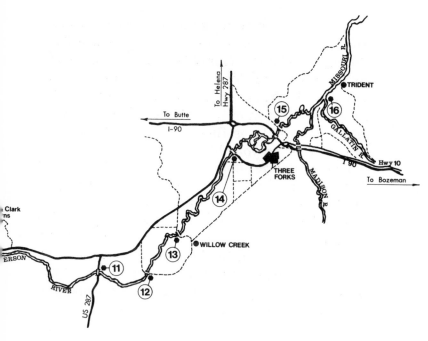

LEGEND

1. 1st Access on Beaverhead
2. Irrigation Diversion Dam
3. Ironrod Bridge
4. Silver Star Bridge
5. Parsons Bridge
6. Parrot Castle Fishing Access
7. BLM Access
8. Kountz Bridge
9. Mayflower Bridge
10. LaHood
11. Sappington Bridge
12. Fishing Access
13. Willow Creek Bridge
14. Hwy. 10 Access
15. Old Town Bridge
16. Headwaters State Park

a half-mile below the fork in the river that leads to the dam. Look for a dirt road on the west side of the river, just before the Ironrod Bridge on Montana 41 at milepost 50. ③ The road parallels the river for about a mile. There's a marvelous variety of water along this section of the Jefferson. Whether your interests lie in lures, flies, or bait, you'll find some of this water to your liking.

Ironrod Bridge affords foot and carry-boat access to the river. The next access point downstream is the Silver Star Bridge, on the south side of the town of Silver Star. ④ You can see it from the road. It's a carry boat access from road to river, and if you are a fisherman afoot, there is easy wading upstream or down at normal summer water levels. A float from Ironrod to Silver Star covers approximately five river miles.

Parson's Bridge lies seven miles below Silver Star ⑤ Take Montana 55 and turn right between milepost 2 and 3 on the road to Waterloo. The bridge is a quarter mile down the road.

Getting a boat to and from the water at Parson's Bridge involves a difficult carry over a fence and down to the water. There is also an irrigation diversion dam there that must be portaged if you're floating through. There is good wading access to the river. The best fly water is downstream; the best lure and bait water upstream.

Parrot Castle Fishing Access ⑥ is the next place where you can reach the river — sort of. It is seven miles downstream from Parson's Bridge, and to get there, you turn east and go 3½ miles on the dirt road near milepost 10 on Montana 55. It is an old fishing access in that you can't drive to the river because of a washed-out bridge over a slough some 200 yards from the river shore. The boat carry takes you over tippy river cobbles, an irrigation ditch, up a steep embankment, down what's left of the aforementioned bridge in what amounts to an amusing exercise in balance and endurance. If you take out here, have a light boat!

Another option is to take out on the other side of the river. It's just a short, steep climb onto a county road. To drive to this access, cross Parson's Bridge and bear left on the Bench Road, which parallels the river. This road also affords good foot access to the river in places, and there is a small block of public (BLM) land that abuts the river 1½ road miles upriver from the old Renova Bridge. ⑦

Parrot Castle Fishing Access is more attractive to the wading fisherman. There is good fly and lure water downstream, and a great bait hole about a half mile upstream, at the base of a chalk cliff.

Kountz Bridge lies approximately four river miles below Parrot Castle. ⑧ You can get a trailer up to the water's edge there, and there is good wading access upriver and down. If you're afoot, I'd call the water within striking distance best-suited to lures or bait. To get to this bridge, turn south on Division Street, in the middle of Whitehall, and drive four miles.

Mayflower Bridge is three miles downriver from Kountz' Bridge. ⑨ Go east on Highway 69 (the main street in Whitehall) and turn south for two miles just before you reach the I-90 underpass, between milepost 4 and 5. You must carry a boat to the water at this point.

Cardwell Fishing Access is approximately six river miles below Mayflower Bridge. You can get a trailer close to the water, but there is no launching ramp. To get there, take Montana 359 south and go through the town of Cardwell. The access is on the south side of the Cardwell Bridge, and for the wading angler, there are fly, lure, and bait opportunities nearby.

FISHING TECHNIQUES

The Jefferson from Twin Bridges to Cardwell represents the swiftest water in the river; hence there are some rainbows there, as well as browns. I'd put the ratio at about seven brown trout to one rainbow. This suggests the wisdom of working midstream stations: the eddies behind emerged rocks and snags, the foot of riffles, and the swift water/slow water "fence" that divides the main current and rotating eddies, as well as classic bank stations. However, the predominance of brown trout also dictates that you will probably get the most action when you fish into the deepest parts of the bank or scrape the bottom of the deepest holes in the river.

If you're a fly fisherman, this section has some nice hatches, and the best of them usually come early or late — before and after the sun hits the water. However, you will not catch the largest fish in the river on top, and you may become annoyed with the incredibly cooperative nature of whitefish. You can avoid most of them if you'll stay away from riffles and the downstream apron below holes, and if you'll use flies size 14 or larger.

During the middle of the day, use streamers and fish them on a sinking or sink-tip line. During late July and most of August, the Jefferson loses a great deal of water to irrigation, and large fish retire to the very bottom of the deepest holes in the river. Even though the water is moving slowly through them, you will need a weighted fly or a sinking line, or both, to get down to these fish.

Although you can find water well-suited to fly fishing at selected spots anywhere along the Jefferson, I'd call the upper reaches of the river, from Twin Bridges to Parrot Castle, the best of the fly water, and the stretch from Parson's Bridge to Parrot Castle the *crème de la crème*.

In a similar vein, if you're a spinfisherman, you'll generally find the best lure water below Parrot's Castle, where the river slows down and becomes more pool than riffle oriented. Wherever you choose to spin fish, the midday action is good on the Jefferson. Concentrate on those parts of pools where the incoming currents flatten out, and work downriver until you can clearly see the entire bottom. Another place to be sure to prospect is anywhere a bank adjoins deep water, and around snags and log jams swept down by spring run-off. One word of warning: these are fishy spots, but they eat lures, so place your casts carefully.

When selecting lures, lean toward spinners and spoons that are slim in profile and heavy in weight. These get the deepest. Use gold or copper when the water is cloudy, and silver during midsummer, when the water is low and clear.

Baitfishing on this section of the Jefferson is generally best when the river is running above normal — roughly from mid-May to the first week of July. Drift-fishing a sculpin by casting it up into a riffle, then floating it down into the heads of holes is the technique that takes most fish, followed by jigging a sculpin across the deeper parts of the apron that forms at the tail end of a pool. Still-fishing with a nightcrawler is an oft-practiced art on this part of the river, but it takes second place to

Flies
Black Maribou
  Muddler
Spuddler
Spruce
Royal Wulff
Elk Hair Caddis
Pale Morning Dun

Lures
Panther Martin
Mepps
Roostertail
Hammered Silver
Hammered Brass

61

drift-fishing with bait. Generally, you can find good worm holes near any bridge.

THE JEFFERSON CANYON

The Jefferson Canyon begins at La Hood ⑩ and ends at the Sappington Bridge on US 287, a distance of approximately 12 river miles. Roughly half of this stretch of river is accessible from Highway 10, although in most places you'll have to cross a railroad track by foot to reach the water.

At milepost 268, near La Hood, there is a two track road that leads down to the water's edge. You can get a boat to the water there. One other access worthy of note is via the settlement known as Sappington. Turn onto Highway 287 South and cross the Sappington Bridge. ⑪ Turn west onto Sappington Road near milepost 84 and drive approximately 1½ miles. When you come to a T in the road, turn left, across the tracks, rather than into Sappington. The road borders the river for about a half mile, but you have to walk across railroad tracks to get to it.

Fishing Techniques

The Jefferson Canyon isn't the prettiest place to fish; railroad tracks run up both sides of the river and so do power poles. There are remnants of past mining operations, and the hillsides are barren and rocky. Midsummer days get blistering hot.

Though the scenery isn't the best, the water in the canyon is attractive, with long, placid pools that follow regular, shallow riffles. The riffles amount to nice water for a fly, and the pools and holes are lure and bait water.

The best fishing is generally from the place where Highway 10 leaves the river to the Sappington Bridge, a distance of about seven miles. The Jefferson wanders away from the highway there, and it offers a good float trip, though you'll have a tricky carry to get a boat to and from the water. Whitefish can be a nuisance in the Canyon, but you can avoid them by using large flies and large lures. If you're interested in whitefish, you can't go wrong with a small, green or brown wooly worm, or a small silver spoon.

If there is one place to prospect for big bragging-size brown trout along this stretch, it is along banks where railroad riprap (large angular boulders placed to prevent roadbed washouts) meets the water. The riprap creates deep rotating eddies, and there always seems to be small, pan-size trout slapping at surface minutiae in them. But if you'll ignore their apparent appeal and go deep with a streamer, a spoon, or a sculpin, you'll tie into some memorable fish.

In the middle of the summer, when the weather starts to get downright hot, fishing drops dead from about 11 until 5 in the afternoon. You might use this time to visit the Lewis and Clark Caverns, a nearby State Park with spectacular underground caves and limestone formations. It's not only an interesting place to see — it's cool in there.

Flies
Girdle Bug
Sandy Mite
Muddler
Spruce
Elk Hair Caddis
Royal Wulff

Lures
Thomas Cyclone
Mepps
Al's Goldfish
Panther Martin
Kamlooper

The Lewis and Clark Caverns were named in honor of those famous explorers. Discovered by a party of hunters in 1892, these caverns comprise one of the largest limestone cave complexes in the Northwest.

SAPPINGTON TO THE THREE FORKS

The Jefferson from Sappington Bridge to the Three Forks amounts to a slow meandering river that winds its way through farmlands and cottonwood bottoms. Aesthetically, it's the most relaxing part of the river to fish, and testimony to the homily that slow water runs deep.

Below Sappington Bridge, the next access is three miles downriver. ⑫ Turn onto the dirt road at either milepost 85 or 86. These roads triangulate after a mile. Go another mile and a half toward the river and you will come to a bridge that is closed to traffic. There's good foot access there, but getting a boat to the water is difficult. There is good boat and foot access on the other side of the bridge. To get there by car (you can cross the bridge by foot) go through the town of Willow Creek and bear right for 3½ miles.

The Cemetery or Willow Creek Bridge lies three miles downstream. ⑬ Turn onto the county roads at either milepost 87 or 89 and go approximately two miles. There is easy carry access to the river on the east side of the bridge and good foot access upstream and down. The water around the bridge is best suited to fly and lure fishing.

Seven miles downriver, Highway 10 crosses the Jefferson west of the town of Three Forks. ⑭ You can carry a boat to the river there, and there is good lure water around the bridge. Highway 10 also provides foot access to two miles of the west side of the river, between milepost 90 and 93. Turn south at the Three Forks interchange, west of town. There is good lure and bait water there.

I-90 crosses the Jeff about a mile downriver, but you're not permitted to park on an Interstate Highway, except for an emergency. The next legal access lies 1½ miles downriver, at the Old Town Bridge. ⑮ Take the gravel road on the north side of the Three Forks interchange east of town, off Highway 10, and go one mile. There is good foot

BASS FISHERMEN!

A few of the oxbow ponds that border the Jefferson between Sappington and Three Forks have bass. They are small by Southern standards, but they provide a change of pace. Most of these ponds have private accesses, but it is not difficult to get permission to fish. Inquire locally.

access there, you can get a boat trailer to the water, and the bridge straddles a classic worm hole. It's a great place for a forked stick, a baited hook, and quiet reflections.

Although there are no more public accesses to the Jefferson below this point (it joins the Madison to form the Missouri three miles downriver), if you are floating, you can take out at the Headwaters State Park, near milepost 3 on the Trident Road. ⑯ Turn left after you cross the Gallatin River. There's an improved launching ramp there and good foot access to the Madison, Gallatin, and Missouri Rivers throughout the Park.

Fishing Techniques

If you yearn to catch a trophy-size brown trout on a fly, the Jefferson from Sappington to the Three Forks is one place that deserves your serious consideration. Fish very early and very late. In fact, the Jeff is a good night-time stream.

You will have to ignore the small trout and whitefish that are forever surfacing to concentrate on going deep with large streamers and sinking line. It will not be the fastest fishing in the world, but whatever ends up on your hook will be substantial.

Fish from the foot of riffles that lie at the head of deep pools, and quarter your cast upstream. Let the line belly out and down, until you estimate your fly is directly across-current from you, then retrieve it in long swift mends of your line. Wiggling your rod tip at the same time will add extra attraction.

Deep water along banks, especially when the river has exposed root structure, or deposited snags, is another fishing hotspot.

Although the Jeff is at its best when the water is fully shaded, I have done well there on late July and August afternoons, fishing a big grasshopper imitation. In this case, cast to the bank and to shadows exclusively. Rises in sunny water will turn out to be small trout or trash fish.

Flies
Maribou Muddler
Spruce
Bighorn Special
Coachman Streamer
Hoppers

Lures
Kamlooper
Wonderlure
Panther Martin
Rapala
Hammered Brass

I have had respectable luck fishing the Jeff with lures in the middle of the day, but morning and especially evening have been the best. Cast to the deep pools, the brush piles, and the shadows, and get the lure down. Brass and copper are the colors to use when the river is at normal levels or cloudy; silver is best during low water. I have also found that solid colors, rather than spots and stripes, on a metallic lure prove more attractive to browns in the Jeff.

Because of the many deep pools, I'd rate this stretch of the river as the best if you are a bait fisherman who likes to still fish. A strip of suckermeat is the bait to use, and you can catch your bait with a worm, which is the reason why you should use suckermeat. Garden hackle, the favorite medium of the still fisherman, lures carp and suckers to your hook, and in this part of the river, they outnumber the trout. If you are a drift fisherman, you'll face the same problem, so use either sculpins or a strip of suckermeat.

FLOATING

While the Jefferson contains its share of floating hazards: wing dams, diversion dams, mid-current snags, and sweepers, the river runs so slowly that you'll have plenty of time to make executive decisions regarding what to do about them. In fact, its leisurely pace suggests few twists to the floater's art.

Although I am not a fan of the canoe as a fishing/floating craft, I would recommend it above other river boats from Twin Bridges to La Hood in midsummer. You will encounter many long flat pools that stretch for a half mile or more. The downstream half of these pools amounts to marginal trout habitat — small trout and a lot of whitefish — and you can move over this water in a hurry with a swift-paddling canoe.

Canoes also make for easy portages to and from the water, and around irrigation dams.

Rafts are probably the least desirable boat on this stretch. They catch wind like a sail, and given those same sluggish pools, if you encounter an upriver wind, you will literally be blown back to where you started. With the exception of the accesses that have rudimentary launching ramps, McKenzies are too heavy to carry to the water. A light jonboat is a reasonable alternative to a canoe, but you'll still do some downriver rowing if a wind comes up. The pools are generally too shallow for an outboard.

Below La Hood, I recommend any river craft to have an outboard, to putt through the slow pools. A light jonboat with a four to six horse engine is ideal since you can carry both to the water.

To approximate the time of your float, figure you will cover one river mile per hour, if you stop and fish the more attractive pools and riffles. If you stay glued to the seat of the boat, figure two miles per hour, if you are not bucking a wind.

If you float the Jefferson around the Whitehall area, you don't have to bring two vehicles to mount

QUICK, HENRY, THE FLIT!

The Jefferson bottomlands, from Sappington to the Three Forks, have a population glut of the fiercest mosquitoes this side of a Florida swamp. They come in sizes small to young eagle, and have an insatiable appetite. Wear longsleeved loose shirts, neutral colors, and fish in the water, rather than rustling up the grass and brush. Above all, bring insect repellent.

It is illegal to use an outboard in excess of 10 horsepower on the rivers of the Missouri Basin.

67

your trip. Bill Peck, at the Alpine Sports Shop, on Whitehall Street, runs a float pick-up service. He drops his car off at your egress point, accompanies you to the beginning of the float, and then drives your vehicle back to his. Median price for this service is $15.00, the charge dependent upon the driving distance the stretch you float is from his shop.

The Madison

The Madison River begins at the confluence of the Gibbon and Firehole Rivers in Yellowstone National Park and ends at the Three Forks of the Missouri, approximately 125 river miles away. That portion of the river lying below Meadow Lake is commonly referred to as the Lower Madison. The river upstream of the lake is called the Upper Madison.

During its journey, the river's bed contours create a variety of stream conditions that touch every stage of water on the move, from pools as slow as honey to wild rapids. This variety of water, and fertility levels that rival Eden, have lead to the Madison's reputation as the top trout stream in the nation.

The Madison has good access along its entire length. Although there is spotty posting of private lands, much of the river is bordered by roads. Removed sections of river have frequent Montana Fish and Game Department fishing access sites and BLM recreation areas. Floating opens up still more water, if you have access to a boat or hire a float guide.

The picture isn't entirely rosy, however. Because of its popularity and accessibility, the Madison receives great fishing pressure. However, I still rate the river as excellent trout water, particularly when you expend the effort to get beyond easy

NOTICE

The Upper Madison River is the subject of an intensive study by the Montana Fish and Game Department. Part of that study is a careful regulation of fishermen and their harvest, including outright river closures, catch-and-release sections, restrictions on floating, the use of bait, and reduced limits. **Check the regulations carfully before you fish the Madison.**

69

Map of the Madison River
from Madison Jct. to Cameron

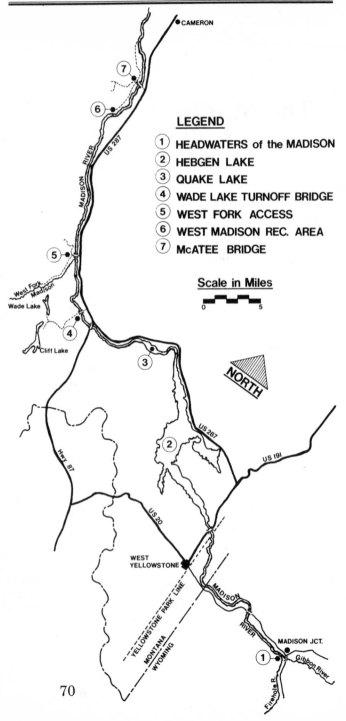

CAMERON

LEGEND

1. HEADWATERS of the MADISON
2. HEBGEN LAKE
3. QUAKE LAKE
4. WADE LAKE TURNOFF BRIDGE
5. WEST FORK ACCESS
6. WEST MADISON REC. AREA
7. McATEE BRIDGE

Scale in Miles

0   5

NORTH

MADISON RIVER

US 287

West Fork Madison

Wade Lake

Cliff Lake

Hwy 87

US 287

US 191

US 20

WEST YELLOWSTONE

YELLOWSTONE PARK LINE

MONTANA

WYOMING

MADISON

RIVER

MADISON JCT.

Gibbon River

Firehole R.

access. It is an infallible rule, no matter where you fish, that the number of strikes you can expect will be directly proportional to your distance from a road.

The Upper Madison is primarily rainbow water. Below Meadow Lake, browns predominate. There are a few grayling in the river from the mouth of O'dell Creek downstream to Meadow Lake, and a chance brookie or two around the mouths of smaller river tributaries. Whitefish are everywhere and easy to catch. Carp and suckers will show up on your hook if you're baitfishing downstream from the Beartraps.

The time of year defines the most effective fishing techniques on the Madison. During June, when the river is bank-full and roily, baitfishing is the most practical approach.

Lures work best from the day the water begins to clear until it nears lowest summer levels, usually the first three weeks of July.

Low, clear water is fly fishing time, a period that commonly runs from mid July through the middle of October, and sometimes later, depending on the severity of the weather.

When water temperatures hover around the 40-degree mark and below...usually by mid-November...trout turn off flies and look to lures and bait. You'll find lures most productive on warm days, and bait's all they will take when there's ice on your guides.

The Madison River was named in honor of President James Madison by the Lewis and Clark expedition of 1804-1806.

THE MADISON:
YELLOWSTONE NATIONAL PARK

The Park section of the river begins at the headwaters of the Madison ① and ends where the river flows into Hebgen Lake, ② a distance of some 20 miles.

That portion of the Madison lying within Park boundaries is limited to fly fishing only. There's some justice in these regulations in that the Madison in the Park is unquestionably the finest fly water on the entire river, with moderate to slow flow velocities and long, sweeping bends that suggest an English chalk stream.

There's public access along the entire river, and except for a short stretch between the Park entrance and Baker's Hole campground, it's always close to a road.

Because of the river's accessibility, overall attractiveness, and Yellowstone as an additional drawing card, the Madison in the Park rates as some of the most heavily fished water in the nation. Trout are alert and shy during the summer months, a condition compounded by the clarity of the water. I have seen rising fish spooked by an approach from 60 feet away coming in from their back side.

SPECIAL PERMITS IN YELLOWSTONE

No fishing license is required in the Park but you must get a special permit, available at every entrance. You can't beat the price; it's free!

Because of lower fishing pressure, the river is at its best during the first two weeks of June and during the month of October, when tourism is down. June is high water time in the West, but even though levels rise to bank heights in June, this section of the Madison remains clear enough for flies. During July and August, you'll find the most action when you fish early or late, the subdued light as much responsible for strikes as feeding patterns.

Late summer and early fall fishing raise one other problem here: an extensive bloom of duck-weed that burps and waves under the surface like giant squirrel tails. At times it makes fishing with anything other than a dry impossible.

Fishing Techniques

Long casts and gossamer leaders are the rule if you're a fly fisherman. A shooting head will increase your reach considerably. Because of the water's overall clarity and depth, floating lines are suitable for wets, nymphs, and streamers.

The fish in the Park can be highly selective, with a decided preference for #16 to #20 nymphs and dries. It's impossible to predict the hatch that may confront you, or the pattern that will match it, but there are some standard flies you should have with you.

I have found it wisest to fish all flies upstream in the Park — dries and nymphs on a dead drift, and streamers and wets quartered so you get some action as the line bellies. If you find the fish are eager and bold, try fishing downcurrent with a #8 muddler behind a #10 green or brown wooly worm on a dropper. Walk down the middle of the river and cast to both banks, imparting plenty of action to the fly. When this trick works, it works incredibly well.

IN YOUR FLY BOX

Dries
Light Cahill
Blue Dun
Adams
Royal Wulff
Goofus Bug

Wets
Leadwing
Coachman
Dark Hendrickson

Nymphs
Montana Nymph
Caddis
Asst. Wooly Worms

Streamers
Muddler
Spruce
Royal Coachman

HEBGEN DAM TO MEADOW LAKE

Virtually all of this section of the Madison is bordered by a highway or dirt road, and sometimes both. Access to the east, or right bank of the river, looking downstream, is via US 287, with many state fishing accesses in those areas where the river wanders away from the road. There's also a BLM recreation area approximately 10 miles south of Cameron. ⑥ North of Cameron, access is most available from the west. Take the first dirt road on the left after leaving Ennis (milepost 1), on Virginia City road (Montana 287).

Downstream from Ennis Bridge, ⑪ access is more limited because the river flows through private lands. There's a state access on Jack Creek Road ⑫ about midway between the bridge and Ennis Lake. To reach other parts of this stretch, you must obtain permission to trespass, or float.

This section of the Madison vies with the Park in its degree of popularity and fishing pressure; consequently, it is the most complexly regulated part of the river and home to some foxy fish. It is often described as "one big riffle," an accurate representation of the conditions you'll encounter. Due to a steep-pitching bed, few meanders, and rather even bottom contours, the river here heads downhill in a bubbly, busy hurry, without any comfortable pools or cutbanks. To the uninitiated, it is puzzling water to fish.

You can solve that puzzle in part by fishing to three lies: behind rocks, along banks, and below broken bars. The rocks are easy enough to find and work, but banks and broken bars present some technical problems.

In order to work a bank effectively, you must fish from the river to the bank. This section of the Madison is swift and paved with rocks as slick as greased cannonballs, making wading difficult and dangerous. If you carpet the bottom of your chest waders, carry a wading staff, and pick your wading

The Madison River
from Cameron to Trident

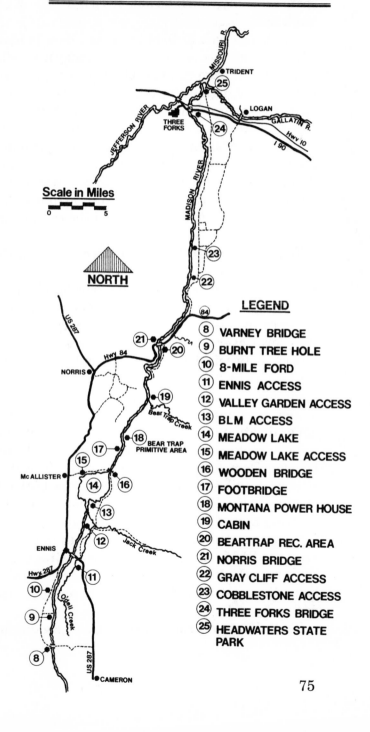

Scale in Miles

0   5

NORTH

LEGEND

8	VARNEY BRIDGE
9	BURNT TREE HOLE
10	8-MILE FORD
11	ENNIS ACCESS
12	VALLEY GARDEN ACCESS
13	BLM ACCESS
14	MEADOW LAKE
15	MEADOW LAKE ACCESS
16	WOODEN BRIDGE
17	FOOTBRIDGE
18	MONTANA POWER HOUSE
19	CABIN
20	BEARTRAP REC. AREA
21	NORRIS BRIDGE
22	GRAY CLIFF ACCESS
23	COBBLESTONE ACCESS
24	THREE FORKS BRIDGE
25	HEADWATERS STATE PARK

75

spots carefully, you'll be able to cast to 50% of the bank area safely.

The tough part of fishing broken bars is identifying them. To the untrained eye, they are indistinguishable from the rest of the river. They are the result of high water deposits of sediment that form underwater bars. When the water drops, the bars act like small dams, until the pressure of the water they're holding back cuts a channel through them. This results in a deep channel of swift water flanked by two pockets of slower water immediately below the bar. Trout station in the slow water to pick off food racing by in the swift channel.

To locate broken bars, you have to watch the water. Look for conflicting currents — water moving downriver slowly and paralleling fast-moving water. Broken bars are also sometimes revealed by a series of small, stationary wavelets that form over the deep channel, the results of friction between the swift water and the bottom.

The overall swiftness of the water in this stretch leads me to conclude that it is generally better suited to spinning than fly fishing. Like any generalization, however, this rule of thumb has some exceptions. I rate the short run from below Hebgen Dam to Quake Lake as good fly water. Below the tailrace that has formed at the outlet of Quake Lake, the river pitches down swiftly, creating rapids, but there are many quiet pockets behind emerged boulders. These conditions prevail until the BLM recreation area at Wall Creek. The river from the BLM campground to Varney Bridge holds the most technically difficult water to fish with a fly rod.

From Varney Bridge downstream, conditions

If you love to eat trout ...think twice before you creel a Madison fish. Their flesh develops a mossy, minty taste in the warmer months that make them less than the best eating. Release them for someone else to catch, and concentrate on small-stream brook trout for your breakfast. Gourmets agree they're the finest table fare of all.

gradually become less difficult, and the stretch from the mouth of O'Dell Creek to Ennis Lake is once again kind to the fly caster. Here the Madison braids around islands and bars, in places breaking into several smaller watercourses. If the magnitude of big, Western water has you down, this is a good place to recuperate.

Fishing Techniques

Here, most of the large trout caught on flies fall prey either to a Muddler Minnow or to one of the many imitations of the giant stone fly (salmon fly). When fishing any sub-surface fly, you'll get the most strikes working it right off the bottom. Use a high-D sinking tip and perhaps a weighted fly as well. Quartering your casts upstream is another trick to getting a fly down deep.

Spinning techniques are similarly keyed to getting down deep, and a lot depends on the lures. Avoid lightweight hardware with a lot of surface area. It sometimes helps to pinch a large splitshot six inches back of your lure when you really want to dredge bottom.

Stations to fish are the same as those for a fly caster, but they will be easier to reach and work with a spinning rod, because the effect of line drag is not so great. A cast that's quartered upstream, then maneuvered past pockets and broken bars will get the most strikes, especially during the part of the retrieve when your lure reverses direction and faces upcurrent.

Because of the scarcity of pools and quiet water on this section of the river, drift fishing is the only baitfishing technique that you'll find productive. It is especially effective used in conjunction with live salmon flies or nymphs in June, during the salmon

Flies
Irresistible
Elk Hair Caddis
Montana Nymph
Muddler
Spruce

Lures
Kamlooper
Krocodile
Mepps Aglia Long
Panther Martin
Doty Raider

fly hatch, but you must work them into or along the bank. That's where the majority of these flies tumble into the river. Hungry trout know this and congregate there. Before and after the hatch, large nightcrawlers are the recommended bait, and drifting them down the swift channels that cut broken bars is the best way to fish them.

Floating

Floatfishing is prohibited on much of the Upper Madison, but the rules seem to change each year, so read the regulations before you launch your trip.

The most floatable water lies downriver of Varney Bridge, with take-out points at the Burnt Tree Hole access, 8 Mile Fork, the Ennis access, the Valley Garden access, and Meadow Lake. Varney to Burnt Tree, Burnt Tree to Ennis, and Ennis to Meadow Lake all make pleasant half-day trips, when you add the time it takes to stop to fish some of the attractive lies.

On the Ennis-to-Meadow Lake float, you'll find the river breaks up into a mini-Mississippi Delta as it nears the lake. Stick with the major river channels that bear east (right looking downriver). When you hit the lake, turn right and follow the shoreline. There is an unimproved launching ramp and BLM access on the southeast corner of the lake. To get there by car, take the Jack Creek Road.

THE BEARTRAP OF THE MADISON

The Beartrap of the Madison begins at Meadow Lake Dam, north of Ennis, ⑱ and ends at the junction of highway 289 with the Madison River, a distance of about 15 river miles. You reach the dam by turning north off US 287 at McAllister, then turning left after you cross the wooden bridge ⑯ that spans the northeast end of the lake.

Roughly two-thirds of the land in the Beartraps is a Primitive Area, where motorized conveyences and appliances (like chainsaws) are excluded. At the flume outlet by the power house and at the end of the Beartraps Wagon Road, signs define the borders of this area.

Land where motor vehicles are permitted includes the Montana Power Road, from the dam to the flume outlet (approximately 1½ miles), and that portion of Beartrap Canyon where the river runs adjacent to Highway 287 (approximately 5 miles). In both sections there is unlimited public access.

Access to the Primitive Area occurs at five points. There is a maintained trail running down the east side of the river the length of the canyon. You enter it from above by going behind the power station. It's about a 50-yard climb, and at present, it takes you through a foreboding array of power installations, but the trail is up there, and no one's been zapped...yet.

Access from the bottom begins at the rock barrier at the end of the wagon road. ⑳ To get on the wagon road, turn off Highway 289 at the BLM recreation area and go by the campground on the dirt road. It's well maintained and poses no threat even to passenger cars.

There is also a trail leading in from the bottom on the west side of the river, beginning at the confluence of Warm Spring Creek with the Madison, at the place where Highway 289 leaves the river. It's easy hiking for two miles, but then the trail gradually disintegrates into a cliffhanger. If you want to get way up in the 'Traps, take the east trail.

WHAT'S IN A NAME?

Legend has it that the Beartrap Canyon got its name from Indians, who considered it the best hunting ground for bear in the area. In fact, black bear are often sighted along this part of the river, especially during berry season.

Two other possible accesses occur on the west side of the river. One begins as a dirt road turning off Highway 289 to the east, ¼ mile south of the stone-block building on the State University Ranch. Follow that road east — it will take you to the rim of the canyon.

A similar road turns off US 287 approximately 3½ miles south of Norris, on the sharp curve that marks the steep climb up Norris Hill.

Both accesses are recommended for pickups or four-bys only, and require about a mile walk down into...then back up out of...the canyon.

Backpacking is an excellent way to fish along the Beartrap Trail. There's a good campsite at the mouth of Beartrap Creek, ⑲ about midway into the Primitive Area, and unique company in the form of Jim Rouse, an old timer and yarn spinner who lives in a cabin there.

Fishing Techniques

Fly fishing is best downstream from Jim Rouse's cabin and from the dam to the powerhouse. The rest of the 'Traps is white and wild, and scree slopes and room-sized boulders next to the shoreline limit back casting. Wading is limited too, because of deep, steep banks and swift water.

I have never done particularly well on dries in the 'Traps. #14 to #8 nymphs and #10 to #4 streamers fished on a hi-D sink tip invariably get more strikes than something floating on top. The nymphs catch the most fish, the streamers the biggest.

Spinning terminal tackle, like fly fishing, is

limited by the nature of the water. Below the cabin, trout prefer spinners that exhibit a lot of flutter and flash at slow speeds. Above the cabin, use heavy, deep sinking spoons and plugs that will sink below the upper, fast current zones.

Above the cabin, baitfishing can be productive. There are deep holes behind the massive boulders that line the shore, and a heavily-weighted bait is the most practical way to fish them. Below the cabin, the Madison is uniformly swift without a great deal of deep water, so generally fly fishing or lure fishing produce best there. In either place, nightcrawlers, sculpins, or live salmon fly nymphs are an equally attractive bait.

Flies
Muddler
Spruce
Wooly Worm
Bitch Creek
Girdle Bug

Lures
Kamlooper
Krocodile
Panther Martin
Rapala
Mirro-lure

Floating

Don't try to float the Beartraps unless you are an expert river rat. The river is wild and dangerous from the powerhouse to Jim Rouse's cabin, and there is one portage around a breathtaking maelstrom rafters call "The Kitchen Sink." Stop and scout ahead when you see a lone, old, nearly-dead pine leaning out over the water on the east bank. There will be a cliff on the west bank and a pronounced necking down of the river ahead.

Below Jim's cabin, the water is suited to the intermediate/novice. Float fishing is popular along the river downstream from the Primitive Area border, because of easy access and easy water. It's also popular with recreational floaters and tubers, so be forewarned on warm summer days to fish early or late.

A straight-through float, from the dam to Highway 289, takes 3½ hours.

THE MADISON MEADOWS

The Madison Meadows begin at the intersection of Highway 289 with the river and end at the Three Forks of the Missouri, approximately 20 miles downstream. Most of the land bordering this section of the river is private, though most landowners will give you permission to trespass if you'll ask.

Public access points include that section of the river bordering the secondary road heading north from the intersection of 289 with the Madison (three miles of river); the Gray Cliff Fishing Access, six miles north of the same intersection (about ¾ of a mile of river frontage); ㉒ the Cobblestone Fishing Access, 3 miles north of Graycliff (¼ of a mile of river frontage); ㉓ the area around the Interstate and Highway 10 bridges, a mile east of the town of Three Forks; ㉔ and that portion of the river lying within the Headwaters State Park (a mile and a half of frontage). ㉕ There's also access on the west side of the river, reached by crossing the Norris Bridge ㉑ and turning north on a dirt road. The road deteriorates the farther north you go, and approximately 6 miles below the Norris Bridge turnoff it leaves the river.

I rate this section as the best on the river for winter fishing and iffy during the warmer months. In the past ten years, thermal pollution from Meadow Lake has encouraged an algae bloom in the Lower Madison...long gossamer strands of green goo that grow from every rock in the river. When you get a rain rise, or when a flood of water is released from the dams above, the algae tears loose, then floating free just under the surface.

When this condition is at its worst, you cannot make a cast with a spinning rod or sinking fly without having the stuff foul your hook, and trout rarely will pick up a fouled lure or fly.

Generally, this condition begins the second week of July, and it is at its worst in mid-September, when cold water kills the algae and it tears loose of its own accord. It is, however, unpredictable. Fishing will be possible, and usually good, when water levels are low, and impossible and poor when the river's up. I have found one reliable test of these conditions: a few exploratory casts from the shore of the Graycliff Fishing Access, will reveal the condition of the river. If you get balled up with goo, fish another section of the river. If your lure stays clean, the rest of the river will offer clean fishing.

Fishing Techniques

Dry fly fishing is tops on this section of the river. The water is smooth, slick, and relatively slow, and there are many pools and eddies. Dries and floating line are one way to beat moss, too, although I've found fish tend to go off feed when the moss is rolling.

The most persistently productive technique is to cast a hopper imitation into the bank when fish are rising at random. When there is a full scale hatch going on, matching the general coloration of the favored fly with a high-floating hair or Wulff pattern is usually enough to fool the trout.

Wets and nymphs are one option when there's no indication of surface feeding activity. Fish them on a high-D sink tip line. When trout aren't feeding on top, the next most logical place to look is right off the bottom.

Large nymphs, from #10's up to hefty #4's will produce the most and largest trout. Smaller trout will take a wet from a #10 to a #14, and you'll also catch a slug of whitefish.

Streamers catch the trophy trout from this section of the river. The biggest I've seen taken has been a four pound brown, and much larger fish have broken off. Work streamers into the bank, or in a long, looping retrieve that dredges the bottom of deep holes.

Flies
Goofus Bug
Elk Hair Caddis
Bitch Creek
Girdle Bug
Muddler

Lures
Panther Martin
Mepps Aglia
C.P. Swing
Kamlooper
Wonderlure

Spinning with lure is a consistent producer of Madison Meadows trout. I recommend six to eight-pound test line. The water is milky, so trout won't be spooked by this weight range, which will pull a snagged lure loose most of the time.

The ability to make long casts is another plus. This is big water, so the more reach you have, the more water you will be able to cover. The most effective cast will be one that quarters upcurrent and then is retrieved along a path that directs the lure through likely lies: pockets behind rocks, holes, eddies, and cut banks. Don't be in a hurry. Let the lure get down deep — where the big ones will be.

Baitfishing is a debatable technique on this stretch of stream. I've found baitfishing to be productive at only two times: during the salmon fly hatch, and in the winter. During the hatch, use salmon fly nymphs or adults. In the winter, the sculpin reigns supreme. Both baits are best fished with a drift rod, bounced right off the bottom and directed through channels and runs.

Floating

Rules, regulations, and difficulty of passage taken into consideration, the Madison Meadows stretch affords the best floatfishing on the entire river. You can launch or take out at any of the access points, and engineer a float that lasts anywhere from an hour to a day. Use the following information as a time guide, but remember that the figures I'm quoting relate to a straight-through float with no stopping to fish. I've found that if you're serious about fishing, you'll want to stop at some of the more attractive holes, at least doubling your time on the river. Another tip — never float barefoot, and watch out for the sun.

Approximate Float Times

Highway 287 — Gray Cliff: 2 Hours; Novice

Gray Cliff — Cobblestone:* 1 Hour; Novice

Cobblestone* — Hwy. 10: 3½ Hours; Intermediate

Hwy. 10 — Three Forks: 2 Hours; Novice

*Overland portage to reach the river

Map of Missouri River

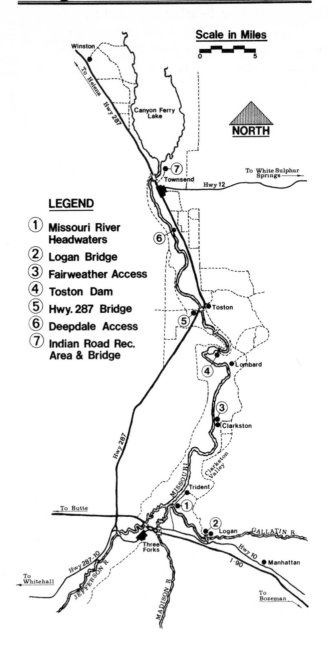

Winston

To Helena

Hwy 287

Canyon Ferry Lake

Scale in Miles

0   5

NORTH

To White Sulphur Springs

⑦
Townsend   Hwy 12

LEGEND

① **Missouri River Headwaters**

② **Logan Bridge**

③ **Fairweather Access**

④ **Toston Dam**

⑤ **Hwy. 287 Bridge**

⑥ **Deepdale Access**

⑦ **Indian Road Rec. Area & Bridge**

⑥

●Toston

⑤

④   ●Lombard

③

●Clarkston

Clarkston Valley

Hwy 287

MISSOURI

Trident

To Butte

①

②   ●Logan   GALLATIN R.

Three Forks

Hwy 287-10   Hwy 10

To Whitehall   I-90   ●Manhattan

JEFFERSON R.

MADISON R.

To Bozeman

The Missouri

The Missouri's headwaters lie at the confluence of the Gallatin, Madison, and Jefferson Rivers, south of the town of Trident. From there, the Missouri flows in a northwesterly direction for approximately forty miles before entering a series of reservoirs, Canyon Ferry being the first.

During its journey, the river spans two contrasting environments: the parched Clarkston Valley and the lush Toston Valley. The dividing point between the two is Toston Dam, a modest irrigation dam that backs up the Missouri for five miles. The dam is located three miles upriver of the town of Toston.

Wherever you join the Missouri, you'll find it to be big water, with a bed that averages over a hundred yards in width. The pitch of the river is gentle, however, and there are no dangerous rapids or white water, save that which tumbles over Toston Dam.

Aesthetically, you may find the Missouri to appear barren, especially on the upper reaches of the river. The tremendous volume of water it carries during the spring run-off scours the riverbed, and when the water recedes, it leaves bare, white cobbles along the shoreline, and bleached midstream bars. It can also be confusing water for the uninitiated to fish, if only because there's so much of it.

Lewis and Clark reached the Three Forks of the Missouri in the spring of 1805. They then scaled the Rockies and explored the Columbia River Basin.

Remarkable facts surrounding their incredible journey: only one man died in their party — of disease; upon their return to St. Louis, the government, in appreciation of their feat, issued both men an unlimited letter of credit, the only one of its kind.

This doesn't suggest, however, that the river is barren of trout too. To the contrary, brown trout — big ones — predominate, followed closely by rainbows. The Missouri also has an enormous population of whitefish, big carp, and suckers that can always be counted on to provide plenty of action if the trout fishing happens to drop off. But that doesn't happen often. In fact, because of its isolation, desolation, and awesome size, the Missouri is actually underfished, and the trout it gives up are, on the average, considerably larger than those caught from other rivers and streams in the area.

The Missouri River, open to fishing all year long, is a reliable place to fish at all times except during spring run-off. There's so much water passing through at this time that the place is unmanageable and unfishable, unless you use a rattlesnake for bait and anchor it in place with a 16-ounce bank sinker. It offers unusually good fishing during the winter and when odd summer weather, like cold snaps and heat waves, put trout down in other places. The reason why this is so, I suspect, is that the volume of water the river carries is less responsive to dramatic temperature changes.

TRIDENT TO TOSTON

The Clarkston Valley lies squarely between Trident and Toston. It amounts to a dry plain set down between two tight canyons. The river runs relatively straight through the canyons, but in Clarkston Valley it develops meanders, and braids around numerous islands and bars.

There are only three convenient public accesses along this entire stretch of river: the Headwaters

Park at the Three Forks, ① Fairweather Fishing Access in the Clarkston Valley, ③ and at Toston Dam. ④

To get to the Headwaters Park, turn north off old Highway 10, three miles east of the town of Three Forks. The Park boundaries and accesses within the Park are well marked.

Getting to Fairweather is more difficult. One route begins just beyond the Headwaters Park, in the middle of the town of Trident. Cross the railroad tracks at the entrance to the Ideal Cement Plant, then bear left. The road will curve around the plant complex and climb sharply. Keep driving north on the main road for about a mile and a half until it T's into another gravel road. Bear left at the T and stay on that main road. It will climb, curve to the left, and level out, the curve to the right, and drop down into Clarkston Valley. The Fairweather Access is plainly marked on the north end of the valley.

Another way into Clarkston is to turn off Highway 10 and head north over the Logan Bridge, immediately west of the town of Logan. ③ This is the same county road that T's into the road from Trident. It is fourteen miles from the Logan Bridge to the Fairweather Access.

To reach Toston Dam, turn north off I-90 west of the town of Three Forks and head toward Townsend and Helena on Route 287. Proceed to milepost 90. There will be a sign on the right that says "Toston Dam." An all-weather gravel road leads in to the dam, a distance of about three miles.

There are other ways to get to the river along this stretch, but you will hardly call them convenient. The Burlington-Northern mainline parallels the river for the whole stretch on the east bank, and the Milwaukee road bed follows the river on the west bank down to the whistle stop of Lombard.

You can drive to Lombard by following the road past the Fairweather Access and bearing left, but it's a chancy venture during or after a heavy rain.

There is also spotty access to the Missouri from the west side of the river, and a substantial amount of BLM (public) land bordering the river, where you won't need permission to trespass. Primitive public roads leading to these places turn off Highway 10 and 287, but to describe the network of roads in this back country and the location of the public lands would be boring and unproductive. If you have a sense of adventure and a pickup truck, write or call the Bureau of Land Management, Granite Towers, Box 30157, Billings, MT 59101 (406) 245-6711, and ask them to send you maps 23 and 33 of the National Resource Lands in Montana. There's also a chance you may be able to find them locally; check with the Montana Fish and Game Dept. (district office), or with the Forest Service in the Federal Building, both in Bozeman. These are truly invaluable maps, full of accurate detail. With them you'll have no trouble getting to the river, and the limited fishing pressure you'll encounter will make the effort more than worth your while.

Fishing with Flies, Lures and Bait

The mighty Missouri dictates an equivalent class of tackle.

The most consistently productive terminal tackle on the Missouri are large #4 to #8 streamers, fished in long, looping retrieves through deep holes and in the pools that form at the foot of riffles. An offbeat way to take a lot of trout with a fly rod is to "troll" while you're float fishing. As the boat drifts along, pay out around twenty-five yards of line upriver, and once it straightens out, jig the fly with measured twitches of your rod tip.

Dries, nymphs, and wets will take Missouri trout, but they will be smaller on the average than what you'll catch on a streamer. You will also hook a few whitefish. Some fishermen consider whitefish a mixed blessing, but if you'll keep an open mind, you'll find them lusty fighters and endearing fish for the simple reason that they cannot turn down a fly.

Hatches on the Missouri often come very early or very late, and when they do, they're usually accompanied by furious top activity that boils the water like a passing shower. Unfortunately, you'll find nine-tenths of the rises will be above whitefish, but again, it's all in whether you enjoy action, whatever the kind. Taking three or four fat trout during an evening rise is good fishing. A bonus of thirty or forty whitefish to fill in the slack between trout has to rate a plus.

The overall pace of the Missouri along this stretch makes it prime water for fly fishing in its entirety, but the braiding and bottomland vegetation around the Clarkston Fishing Access lead me to prefer that spot over all others, not because there are more fish but because of the beauty of the surrounding country.

Spinfishing with lures likewise is most productive with long-range tackle. You will catch the biggest, if not the most fish, using ½- to ⅝-ounce spoons, spinners, and plugs. Work them just off the bottom in the river's deeper holes and along the foot of riffles and bars.

Flies
Maribou Muddler
  Big Horn Special
Wooly Worm
Montana Nymph
Goofus Bug

Lures
Rapala
Kamlooper
Krocodile
Panther Martin
Hammered Gold

91

If larger Missouri trout refuse to cooperate, try using small ¼- to ⅜-ounce spinners. Fish them along cutbanks and in the smallish pools created by railroad riprap where the tracks parallel the shore. These places are always good for whitefish, and trout up to twelve inches.

Beyond the observation that the farther you get from easy access, the better you'll usually find the fishing, there are no especially good — or bad — sections of the Missouri for spinning with a lure. It is uniformly good fishing water.

Baitfishing gets results on the Missouri all season long. Unlike some other area streams that get clear as glass, the Missouri remains on the milky side, even during low, midsummer water conditions. If you like to work with a moving bait, drift-fish the channels that form in the aprons below big pools. Other prime places to plumb are holes on the outside of the river meanders.

The bait for drift fishing in the Missouri is the sculpin, known locally as "bullhead" (though it isn't related to real bullheads). Rig the bait so it bounces bottom and work it through each drift by gently jigging your rod tip. This imitates the bottom-darting habits of the live fish.

The Missouri also provides ideal still fishing in the great swirling pools that form on sharp bends of the river. The favored bait here is a 2-inch strip of sucker meat, largely because it is not attractive to suckers, carp, or whitefish, which will steal a worm bait with annoying regularity.

If you are something of a practical joker, however, take a friend fishing, bait him up with a worm, and don't tell him there are carp in the river. At some point, a ten to fifteen pound tank is going to grab hold of that bait and just walk away. I have generated countless big-ones-that-got-away stories among my friends in just that manner.

Floating from Trident to Toston

The Missouri affords the finest floating in this area. It's an ideal way to get to otherwise unreachable parcels of the river, and the gentle pitch of the river bed creates conditions safe enough for anyone's first float.

You'll find use for an outboard on the Missouri, unlike other rivers in south central Montana. The river is big enough and deep enough to navigate under power, and you'll probably want to chug on through some of the longer, slower pools.

Without an outboard, a straight-through float from Trident to Toston will take more than a day. Toston Dam backs up dead water for some five miles, and rowing or paddling is slow going. Another caveat: It is possible to chug back upriver under power, avoiding the need for a pick-up vehicle downstream, but it takes a practiced eye at reading water, and usually some propeller protection as well. Unless you're good at this game, plan on working with the current, not against it.

Pickup points are, for all practical purposes, at the Clarkston Access and Toston Dam. Roads on the west side of the river do not lead right to the water's edge. If you pick up your boat on this side of the river, you'll have to carry it and your gear over the railroad right away. If you choose to take your boat out at Clarkston, note that there is no way to back a trailer into the water. The boat must be lifted up a steep six-foot bank. There is a primitive boat ramp at Toston Dam, behind the gate-tender's house.

The float from Trident to Toston Dam will take a

full day, and that's without a great deal of dallying around choice fishing holes. A better way to make this run is to make it an overnighter, camping at the Clarkston Access, which lies just about midway along the float. If you float from Trident to Clarkston, plan on four to six hours on the river, depending on how often you stop to fish from the shore.

TOSTON DAM

Toston Dam deserves special mention because it creates a unique fishing opportunity. Although trout do not have the same biological need to migrate as salmon do, they seem to have the same urge, and Toston Dam acts as a block to their migration upriver. Rainbows start to gang up at the foot of the dam around mid-April, and browns congregate there toward the end of August. Fishing for trophy-class trout is the main attraction, but there's extra pleasure in just watching these huge spawners try to vault the 20-foot high falls. Trout in the two to five pound class are common, and you'll often see an eight to ten pounder try to match his sleek strength against the cascading water.

What's the trick to tying into one of these wall mounts? For a starter, you've got to think like a steelhead.

Spawning trout do not exhibit the same feeding patterns as trout during normal times. In fact, they feed seldom, if at all. They will strike at a fly, lure, or bait, but it's usually the result of anger not hunger. Hence, it's the intimidating terminal tackle that will take the most fish.

Fly fishing is almost exclusively a matter of sinking or sinktip lines and large bright flies. You will see fish rising in the tailrace, but most of them will be carp, whitefish, and suckers. Trout will roll every once in a while, but it seems to be more a matter of exercise than of searching for food. I've never taken a trout on a dry below Toston Dam.

Because of relatively high banks, swift water, and the need for casting reach, you'll find fishing easier and more productive from a small boat. Anchor it in midstream and fish downcurrent and across current, working your fly in long, jerky, looping retrieves. Stay well back from the boils at the base of the Dam — they're dangerous — and use a cheap cement block for an anchor. The rocks below the dam apron are sharp and angular, and they eat conventional anchors.

Spinning with lures gets the best results when you use large, bright spoons and spinners. I strongly favor lures with fluorescent dots or stripes. They're the same color as roe, and for some odd reason, roe is one natural bait that a spawning trout will take.

The most successful retrieve will be the one that incorporates the most action, yet remains deep, barely scraping bottom. These fish have to be teased into striking, and the best way to do that is to put the same arrogant lure in front of their noses again and again and again. Don't do a lot of moving about in an attempt to cover a lot of water, a wise tactic under normal conditions; but it's counter-productive when you're dealing with spawners. Stay put and stay determined, and you'll catch your fish.

Bait fishing has a few different twists too. Rig a snelled #10 hook eight inches above a heavy-

Flies
Coachman Streamer
Spruce
Sofa Pillow
Mickey Finn
Girdle Bug

Lures
Kamlooper
Krocodile
Wonderlure
Little Jewel
Panther Martin

enough sinker to hold bottom. If you can find some cured roe, form it into a ball around the hook and hold it in place with a thin nylon or cheesecloth sack, tied off at the top of the hook with sewing thread. If you have no roe, thread small pieces of worm on the point and bend of the hook, so all of the metal is covered, but there is no excess worm hanging out.

Cast well into the current and keep your rod in your hand at all times. When a spawner takes a bait, he does it ever so gently, and he doesn't hang around and gnaw on it. You will feel only the barest nibble, almost like something brushing against your line. When you suspect a trout is mouthing your bait, strike and set hard and fast. It's more than rare for these big spawners to hook themselves.

Don't expect fishing below the dam to be fast. It's a good day when you take two or three fish. But the size of the trout that turn up on the end of your line will more than compensate for numbers. If you have a hankering for a wall mount, this is one of the best places in the state to go.

TOSTON DAM TO CANYON FERRY LAKE

This stretch of the Missouri flows through the Toston Valley, a broad basket of fertile farmland. The river banks are stable and thickly-vegetated, and as a result there are more riffles, pools, and pockets per mile of stream than there are above the dam. In general, it is more enjoyable, more fishable, and more understandable water than from Trident to Toston.

There is free public access along the Toston Dam

road for approximately two miles downstream of the dam. Large boulders in the stream bed produce interesting fishing there. The dam road then wanders away from the river, and the next point of access occurs at the Highway 287 Bridge, ⑤ west of the town of Toston.

Downstream of this point there's little public access to the shore. There's some Burlington-Northern right of way between milepost 83 and 84, and about a half mile of frontage along the Deepdale Fishing Access, seven and a half miles west of the Toston bridge. ⑥ Five and a half miles west of Deepdale, you'll find the Indian Road Recreation complex, where Highway 287 again crosses the Missouri. ⑦ The State also manages a large tract of public land that begins approximately a half mile west of the Indian Road Access. It lies to the northeast of Highway 287 and provides access both to the river and to the upper reaches of Canyon Ferry Lake. In addition, there is lake and river access from Indian Road. Turn north just before you cross the bridge.

This tract of land is managed more for wildlife, especially waterfowl, than for trout and fishermen, so there are some restrictions on where you can go and what you can do. Read the posted regulations carefully. Their purpose is to preserve nesting habitat and to protect nesting birds.

Within these strictures, however, the angling along the short stretch from the Indian Road Recreation Area to the mouth of the Missouri where it enters Canyon Ferry is excellent. In the spring and fall, spawning rainbows and browns abound. In midsummer, fish run up the river to escape the heat generated over the shallow upper end of the lake.

With the exception of the access points as listed, the rest of the Missouri from Toston Dam to Canyon Ferry Lake, is bordered by private lands, so you will have to get permission to fish there. But this is not hard to come by — the folks in the Toston Valley are cordial people.

Fishing with Flies, Lures, and Bait

The meanderings of the Missouri here make intimate pockets, riffles, and pools that are fishable with mid-range 6- & 7-weight fly rods and lines. However, there's ample big water to contend with, so if you have the option, take your 8- or 9-weight tackle as well.

Whatever rods and reels you take, avail yourself of the adaptability afforded by both a floating and sinking line. This stretch of the river has some nice hatches, but you'll still take the most trout by fishing deep.

The most productive place to cast a line is usually into willow-lined banks. Trout station there to pick off the frequent caddis hatches and a host of terrestrials: grasshoppers, beetles, ants, and so forth. You'll find the fewest trout in the middle of the river, especially when the water is flat and featureless.

You will catch the largest fish with some sort of sculpin imitation fished behind rocks and riffles, and into the bank. In midsummer, try fishing a sculpin imitation dry, or use a grasshopper pattern.

If you note trout rising to a hatch, first try a light-colored, high-floating hair fly like an Irresistible or a Royal Wulff. I've found the trout in this part of the Missouri to be suckers for bright flies, even when they are gulping down dark-colored insects.

In the absence of surface activity, or interest in conventional streamers, try rigging a large nymph on a dropper and fish it ahead of a streamer. Work it on a dead drift until the line bellies with current drag, then retrieve it as you would a streamer.

If you're spinning with lures or fishing with bait, concentrate on river bends. It is their nature to bear the hydraulics: holes, eddies, and channels that are especially well suited to spinning equipment. If you're lure fishing, work the great swirling holes, which have the largest trout, with large, heavy spoons. If you get no results with this tactic, do an about face and plumb fast, bubbly riffles with a small spinner. They are nearly a sure bet for whitefish and pan-sized trout.

If you are a bait fisherman and familiar with drift fishing techniques, work a sculpin through the swift water at the head of holes, down into their depths. If you prefer to still fish, anchor a strip of sucker meat where fast river water and calm back water meet over a deep hole. On a per-fish basis, there have probably been more Missouri trophy trout taken with this simple approach than with all the feathers and hardware on local tackleshop walls.

Flies
Maribou Muddler
Hoppers
Elk Hair Caddis
Girdle Bug
Wooly Worm

Lures
Mepps Aglia
Panther Martin
Pearl Dardevle
Rapala
Wonderlure

Floating from Toston to Canyon Ferry

You'll find put-in/take-out points south of the Toston Bridge, at the Deepdale Fishing Access, at the Indian Road Recreation Area, and near the mouth of the Missouri. All four points will handle a light, trailered boat. It's possible to put a boat in just below Toston Dam, but you'll have to carry it a short distance to the water.

There's also a rather devious route into the head of Canyon Ferry Reservoir. After you cross the

Highway 287 Bridge north of Townsend, count the dirt roads leading off the highway on the right. Take the third dirt road (between mileposts 75 and 76). Bear left as the road divides and follow it to the end. It dead-ends at a parking lot of sorts, by a slow-moving backwater.

The other trick is finding that backwater from the river. As soon as you round the last bend and the lake comes into view, get into the pond-like backwater on the left (looking downriver). It's about a quarter mile upriver from the lakeshore. You'll be fighting a slow current to get to the parking lot. It's about a quarter mile up the backwater, and your car will be in plain sight.

Wherever you choose to float, the river is safe, even for the novice river rat, all the way from Toston Dam to Canyon Ferry. The float from the dam to Toston Bridge takes a half day. Toston Bridge to Deepdale, and Deepdale to the Indian Road Access each takes a full day when you add a few stops to fish the more inviting holes. Indian Road to Canyon Ferry is a short float — less than an hour if you float straight through.

Float fishing from Toston Dam to Toston Bridge, and Indian Road to Canyon Ferry, is especially good in April, August and September, due to the spawners that bank up in this section of the river.

The Yellowstone

The Yellowstone River is the longest free-flowing river in Montana. It begins at the outlet of Yellowstone Lake, in Yellowstone National Park, and flows in a northerly direction to the town of Livingston. At Livingston, it turns east and rambles on for three hundred miles before joining the Missouri near the North Dakota/Montana border.

Between the towns of Big Timber and Columbus, the Yellowstone changes its personality, leaving the mountains and entering the High Plains. Below this point, it supports populations of warm water fish: carp, ling, goldeye, sauger, paddlefish, catfish, sturgeon, and an occasional northern pike. Upstream, it is home to coldwater fish: brown, brook, cutthroat, and rainbow trout; whitefish and suckers.

The Upper Yellowstone, from an angling point of view, is best discussed in four sections: the Yellowstone in the Park, Yankee Jim Canyon, Paradise Valley, and from Livingston to Big Timber. Each parcel of river differs in swiftness, geography, and the preferences of the trout that live there.

THE YELLOWSTONE IN THE PARK

The Yellowstone flows tranquil and smooth from its headwaters at Fishing Bridge ① to

101

Map of Yellowstone River

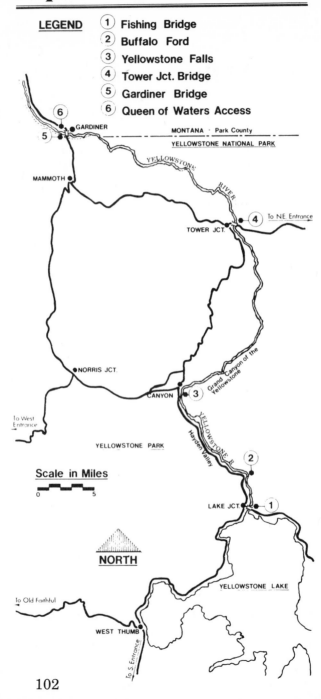

LEGEND
1. Fishing Bridge
2. Buffalo Ford
3. Yellowstone Falls
4. Tower Jct. Bridge
5. Gardiner Bridge
6. Queen of Waters Access

MONTANA - Park County
YELLOWSTONE NATIONAL PARK

GARDINER

YELLOWSTONE RIVER

MAMMOTH

To N.E. Entrance

TOWER JCT.

NORRIS JCT.

Grand Canyon of the Yellowstone

CANYON

YELLOWSTONE R.

Hayden Valley

To West Entrance

YELLOWSTONE PARK

Scale in Miles
0   5

NORTH

LAKE JCT.

To Old Faithful

YELLOWSTONE LAKE

WEST THUMB

To S. Entrance

Yellowstone Falls, ③ at the beginning of the Grand Canyon of the Yellowstone, a distance of approximately thirteen river miles. The river is often in sight of the road and always within easy walking distance. There are some closures to fishing along this stretch of the Yellowstone — an attempt to keep conflicts between people and wildlife at a minimum — but if you are a fly fisherman, the water where angling is permitted is the easiest stretch of the entire river to fish. Currents are gentle, the water is clear and wadable, and there's a huge population of cooperative Yellowstone cutthroat trout.

Conditions there are well-suited to rods and lines in the 6-weight range, and there is no real need for sinking tips or shooting heads. Evening hatches come with the regularity of sunrise, and when the trout aren't topping out, you can usually catch all you want on a nymph. Conditions are so perfect there that Stu Apte, a friend of mine and an internationally-known angler and writer, called the stretch around Buffalo Ford ② "the best place in the world to go if you've never caught a trout on a fly."

The Grand Canyon of the Yellowstone lies below the awesome falls, and from the Canyon to tower Junction, ④ the Yellowstone is in many ways the opposite of the river above. Access is difficult, and sometimes impossible, because of the steep canyon walls. The road wanders far from the river — up to five miles in some places — and secondary road accesses are sparse. Because the river is so difficult to reach, fishing pressure is virtually non-existent along this stretch once you venture beyond the few access points. Be forewarned, however, that fishing the Yellowstone back country is a young

Flies
Montana Nymph
Girdle Bug
Olive Wing Dun
Goofus Bug
Maribou Muddler

Lures
Thomas Cyclone
Roostertail
Panther Martin
Doty Raider
Mepps Aglia

person's game.

Because of the effort required to reach and fish the Yellowstone at this point, I recommend a blend of tackle that's comparable to that which you'd use backpacking; a combination spin/fly pack rod, a light spinning reel, a fly reel with two arbors (one loaded with floating line and the other with sinking line), and a good selection of both lures and flies. The one change I recommend in the basic backpacking package is in the weight of lures and size of flies. This is big, powerful water, with deep pools and swift rapids punctuated by massive boulders. To get down to the fish with hardware, you'll need lures in the ½- to ⅝-ounce range. In terms of flies, if the cutthroat there aren't taking dries, I've had the most luck using large #6 to #10 nymphs fished deep on a hi-D sink-tip line.

Below Tower Junction, the Yellowstone picks up the water from the Lamar River. It broadens its bed and becomes less tortuous, dancing over cobbles and boulders on a relatively straight path down through Black Canyon. Deep pools are less common; riffles predominate, and the river at this point is best suited to flies.

Dries seem to be most appealing to trout when fished upriver and into the calm pockets of water that form behind rocks. Wets and nymphs are best fished by quartering a cast downcurrent, into these same pockets of water, then letting the current carry line and fly in a long, looping swing.

Streamers begin to pack some appeal as you approach the Park border, largely because brown trout and rainbow begin to become part of the trout population. Fish your streamers the same way as wets and dries, but give them a choppy, jerky retrieve.

Spinning with lures will take trout along this part of the river, and the most successful hardware is usually a ⅜-ounce silver spinner. Work the pockets behind boulders and cover a lot of water, rather than concentrating on one spot.

Although the geography of the Yellowstone River and Valley below Tower Junction is more gentle than upstream, the hike in and the swift water make fishing there demanding sport — even more so than packing in to a high country lake, because you'll be bucking a current all day long. I highly recommend that you evaluate the conditions you'll encounter before you go, from some spot that's easy to reach: from the Gardiner Bridge, from the bridge east of Tower Junction, or at the Grand Canyon of the Yellowstone. In many ways, the Yellowstone between the Falls and Gardiner is the same as when it was first discovered. The quality of the fishing is excellent, but fishing there is not an adventure to be undertaken lightly.

GARDINER THROUGH YANKEE JIM CANYON

There is good access to the Yellowstone from Gardiner through Yankee Jim Canyon. US 89 borders the river on the east, and a gravelled country road borders the river on the west. There are bridges across the river at Gardiner, ⑤ Corwin Springs, ⑧ and Carbella, ⑩ at the foot of Tom Miner Basin.

Above Yankee Jim Canyon, the Yellowstone is shallow, wide, and relatively swift. Rainbows predominate, followed by brown trout and cutthroat. Rainbows and cutthroat keep to the fast water

The Yellowstone River from Gardiner to Livingston

LEGEND

- ⑤ Gardiner Bridge
- ⑥ Queen of Waters Access
- ⑦ Carbella Access
- ⑧ Corwin Springs Bridge
- ⑨ Point of Rocks Bridge
- ⑩ Carbella Bridge
- ⑪ Emigrant Bridge
- ⑫ Paradise Fishing Access
- ⑬ Loch Leven Fish. Access
- ⑭ Mill Creek Bridge
- ⑮ Mallard Rest
- ⑯ Pine Creek Bridge
- ⑰ Hwy. 10 Bridge

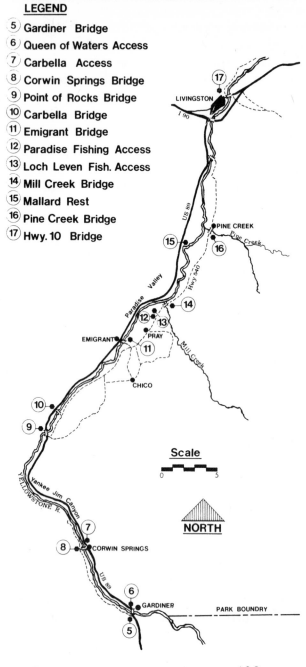

between river meanders and pools, and brown trout reside in deeper, calmer water.

Recognizing where each type of trout is likely to lie is one of the secrets to success on the Yellowstone, for it's a reliable rule of thumb that rainbows and cutts prefer one kind of terminal tackle, and browns another. This is also true of other rivers in the area, but not to the same extent as on the Yellowstone.

Fly fishing in the faster water for rainbows and cutts finds insect imitations most productive, with nymphs outstanding. Use either a weighted fly, or a sink-tip line. The water in this portion of the river isn't deep, but it is swift, elevating a nymph above feeding zones. Trout here will take a dry, but dries are difficult to keep afloat because of the swift water.

In the slower pools, it's easy to keep a dry afloat, but you'll find that only dinky trout will be interested in it. These places are the lair of big brown trout, which strongly favor a streamer above all other flies. Fish streamers weighted, or with a sink-tip line.

Flies
Maribou Muddler
Spuddler
Spruce
Montana Nymph
Wooly Worm

Lures
Kamlooper
Krocodile
Wonderlure
Rapala
Fjiord Spoon

Spinning lures follow this same pattern. Use flashy gold and silver spinners in the fast water, and heavy gold and silver spoons in the slow water. Another tip: lures with dots or a stripe of fluorescent red are uncommonly attractive to browns.

Yankee Jim Canyon, named for an old trapper and mountain man who lived in the area, amounts to stretches of swift, wild water, with deep pools strung between them like pearls on a necklace. The power and depth of the river here make it a poor bet for fly fishing, unless you adapt to the conditions with deep-sinking line and a heavy rod. You will take some small rainbows and cutts fishing a dry through the rips and eddies close to the bank, but this is really brown trout water — big ones at that, and they just don't come easy when you're fishing with feathers, even with big, weighted streamers.

Yankee Jim is better suited to lures and bait. In the former category, start off with a ½-ounce or a ⅝-ounce spoon that is narrow in profile and high in specific density. These are the characteristics that will get you down to the bottom of the big pools, where the big trout watch and wait. If you don't have such a lure in your tackle box, at least weight your heaviest spoon with a pinch of cannon ball split shot. Joining two light spoons together with split rings is another trick that creates a deep-sinking lure with unique action.

The best bait in Yankee Jim is a large fresh or frozen sculpin. Fish it on a #6 or #4 double needle hook, below enough weight to bring the bait down to the point where it ticks bottom. The trick to fishing a sculpin — the best all-around bait on the Yellowstone — is to keep it moving and active, appearing to dart from rock to rock. Still-fishing even a live sculpin will prove unproductive and frustrating. Live sculpins immediately dive for the closest crevice, and they'll snag you on every cast.

One trick worth practicing when drift-fishing a sculpin is to sever its spine midway between tail and head. This limbers up the tail and the sculpin appears to be swimming, thus curing the "stiffs" common to frozen bait.

CARBELLA BRIDGE TO LIVINGSTON

From Carbella Bridge to Livingston, the Yellowstone flows through Paradise Valley, an aptly named place of exceptional beauty. Green, manicured farm and ranch lands gently dish up to meet towering mountains — Emigrant Peak, the third highest mountain in the state — has a cap of snow year round, and the river meanders past towering cottonwoods and around numerous islands.

Although much of the abutting acreage is private land, there is good access to the river. US 89 touches the Yellowstone on the west side at points all the way down to Livingston, and Route 540 borders the river down to Emigrant Bridge, ⑪ on the east. In addition, there are bridges at Point of Rocks, ⑨ just below Yankee Jim Canyon, at Emigrant, near Mill Creek, at Pine Creek, ⑯ and just below Allen's Spur (Carter Bridge). Along US 89, there are Fish and Game accesses at milepost 42, at Emigrant, at Corwin Springs, and one mile north of Gardiner. On Route 540, there are two fishing accesses south of the Mill Creek Bridge.

In Paradise Valley, the Yellowstone conforms to a riffle-pool scheme of stream flow. Although this pattern is on a grand scale and sometimes hard to perceive, it makes this section of river a favorite for fly fishing because the water is relatively easy to read and interpret and because the river's pace is well suited to the limitations of a fly rod.

As is the case above Yankee Jim Canyon, rainbows, cutts, and whitefish are most commonly taken from the shallower, faster sections of the Yellowstone. If you're after these fish, use dries and small nymphs in the bubbly water above and below deep pools and river bends. The big browns

Rules of Thumb on the Yellowstone

Spring: Fish the riffles and side-channels for rainbow.

Midsummer: Fish toward brushy banks and dredge deep holes.

Late Summer: Fish the heads and tails of pools.

Fall: Fish the riffles and, side-channels for brown trout.

favor the deep, swirling water near the head of pools and on the outside of river bends. The pools that lie ahead of and behind river riprap are other favorite hang-outs.

If you are good at reading water, you can take both big rainbows and brown trout by fishing the holes below midstream riffles. The places are tough to pick out, and in the West, the ability to recognize them separates the merely good from the truly excellent angler. Look for fast-moving, shallow, and often bubbly water that abruptly slows down, taking on a slick, oily appearance. This water will not be flat calm as in the tail end of a pool. It will be bouncy, but it will still have a tranquil, swirling look. Trout like to station just downstream of the point where the bubbly current enters the hole and slows.

Flies
Girdle Bug
Coachman Trude
Grant's Stone
Fly
Hoppers
Maribou Muddler

Lures
Doty Raider
Little Jewel
Mepps Aglia
Panther Martin
Goldfish

When you are fishing for big trout, you'll get the best results using sinking line and large flies. Use big nymphs until the Yellowstone reaches normal summer levels; then concentrate on streamers. In August, you can take trophy-class fish dry by fishing a large, brown grasshopper imitation into the bank.

Spinfishing with lures will catch rainbows, cutts, and whitefish in the riffles, if you'll use light gold and silver spinners. In the deeper pools, switch to heavy spinners and spoons. Small minnow plugs like the Rapala also work on the Yellowstone. They take fewer fish than spinners or spoons, but the trout they catch will average larger.

Whatever kind of water you're on, the most successful retrieve will always come from a cast that has been quartered upstream and allowed to sink so that it's barely scraping bottom before you set the lure to motion. When the cast is correctly executed, the current will carry the lure downstream of your position, so that at the end of the retrieve, your line will quarter downstream. The lure will also go through a "turnaround," a reversal of direction as it is first swept downstream, then drawn against the current as you take in line. You'll find 50% of your strikes will occur within seconds of that "turnaround."

Baitfishing on the Yellowstone holds up well all year long, though the preferred baits change with the season. If you are a still-fisherman, or long to see success for someone who is unfamiliar with more sophisticated fishing techniques, rig up with a #6 snelled baitholder hook a foot above a ½-ounce bell sinker. Find a slow-moving, deep hole where you can't see bottom — there are a lot of them near bridges and where the river bends next to the highway. Cast a night crawler into the hole when the water is muddy or cloudy, or a strip of sucker meat when the water is clear, and you'll very likely tie into a respectable trout.

If you are a drift-fisherman, live salmon flies are the top bait when this famous hatch is on. Before and after the hatch, when the water is clear, sculpins will catch the most fish, and in late July and August, large brown grasshoppers, known locally as "clackers," are in demand. And here's a puzzler: yellow-bodied, red-legged grasshoppers won't catch half the fish that clackers will!

Floatfishing

The plentitude of accesses and the gentle pitch of the riverbed in Paradise Valley make it an ideal place for floatfishing. While I don't recommend it for a boatload of fishermen who have never floated

The Yellowstone River from Livingston to Big Timber

LEGEND

- ⑰ Hwy. 10 Bridge
- ⑱ U.S. 89 Bridge
- ⑲ Sheep Mountain Access
- ⑳ Springdale Bridge
- ㉑ Grey Bear Access
- ㉒ Big Timber Bridge

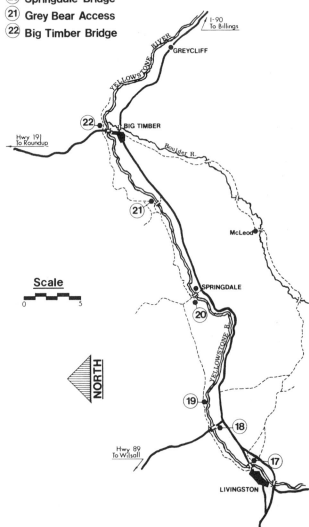

before, if you've had a little experience with the way a river works, the Yellowstone here is a perfectly safe float. Trips can be mounted that range from an hour to a day, and all the pick-up and drop-off points can be reached by conventional transportation and light trailers.

One potential danger you should be aware of, however, resides in several side-channels in the form of irrigation diversion dams. If you stick to the main river, you won't have to confront them. If you get off into a side channel, be cautious about long, slow pools.

LIVINGSTON TO BIG TIMBER

Interstate 90 follows the Yellowstone from Livingston to Big Timber, but it touches the river in only a few places. The primary access points include the 9th Street Bridge, in the town of Livingston; the old Highway 10 Bridge, east of town ⑰ (across the railroad tracks and turn right); the US 89 Bridge on the road to White Sulpher Springs; ⑱ the Sheep Mountain Fishing Access, four miles east; ⑲ the Springdale Bridge, north of milepost 354; ⑳ the Grey Bear Fishing Access, near milepost 363; ㉑ and at the Big Timber Bridge, north of town on the road to Roundup. ㉒

There's additional foot access from Interstate 90 along several stretches of Burlington-Northern right of way that you can see from the road, and from numerous private accesses — dirt roads that turn off the highway and lead down to the river. You have to get land-owner permission to use these private roads, but those who ask are seldom refused.

Approximate Float Times

Point of Rocks — Emigrant: Full Day

Emigrant — Mallard's Rest: Full Day

Pine Creek — Carter Bridge: Half Day

Carter Bridge — 9th St. Bridge: ⅓ Day

From a purely technical point of view, this stretch of the Yellowstone is generally better suited to lure and bait fishing than to fly fishing. It is big, swift water, lacking the comfortable pockets and inviting riffles that most fly anglers prefer to work.

Also, it is underfished water. Perhaps because of the technical difficulties of casting over powerful currents, the fishing pressure from Livingston to Big Timber is light; as a result, there's a substantial population of trout, especially big browns. You'll also find the whitefish big and prolific here, offering excellent winter fishing.

The most practical approach to fly fishing is to use a weight-forward sinking or sink-tip line, and a large streamer. I favor lightly-dressed streamers like the Spruce, Bighorn Special, and Silver Doctor in this stretch because they sink more quickly than even a weighted Muddler, which has the added buoyancy and bulk of a deer-hair body.

When you're fly fishing, you must pick your water carefully. This section of river is kindest to those who can cast well and far, and who know how to read water. I get the most reliable results fishing below broad, shallow riffles that tumble into deep holes. Cast parallel to the riffle and let the current seize your line. As it loops out and swings downstream, twitch the rod tip. You won't have to take in line; as a matter of fact, if it's possible, pay out line as you twitch so that the fly drifts down into the hole. When your line straightens out, retrieve the fly by stripping in line erratically and cast again over the same water. After three casts, move another six feet out onto the bar that forms the riffle and resume casting. Current vectors will carry your fly into new stations.

Weather and the Yellowstone

Fishing is best on a cloudy day.

When it's bright and clear, fish deep.

Don't give up when it starts to rain.

114

If you prefer to fish with nymphs or dries, try working them over the shallow apron that forms on the tail end of large pools. Drop your cast up-river of the point where the bottom fades from view. The fish that you catch will probably be 10- to 14-inch trout and whitefish, when you work a shallow apron in this manner. This part of the Yellowstone will give up large trout to a dry, but they are generally caught in August and September, by fishing a grasshopper or dry Muddler into the bank.

Spinning with lures is the most effective approach to swift, deep water. I recommend heavy spoons or sinking plugs, since they get down deeper than spinners. Quarter your casts up-current and direct your retrieve so it passes breaks in the current: boils, eddies, and breakwaters, where trout can fin in relatively quiet water. It is a truism of trout fishing everywhere, but especially so here, that the ability to perceive places where trout are likely to lie, and to place a cast that puts a lure right on them, is far more important to fishing succes than the quality or kind of tackle used.

Baitfishing is a productive technique all year long below Livingston. During the dry summer, the river above town is so clear that the appeal of bait is marginal at best, but downstream the water always stays slightly cloudy. Sculpins are the best bait for drift-fishing. Night crawlers and strips of sucker meat work best if you're a still-fisherman. Whatever your style, concentrate your efforts at big holes on river bends. Drift a sculpin into them from the riffle above, or still-fish in the middle of them. If you're a still-fisherman, hang on to your rod. I was once fishing with an old friend who dozed off, in the afternoon sun, by a big hole on the

Flies
Maribou Muddler
Spruce
Wooly Worm
Bitch Creek
Hoppers

Lures
Rapala
Krocodile
Little Jewel
Pearl Dardevle
Panther Martin

Yellowstone, when a monster simply ran off with the works — rod, reel and tackle.

Floatfishing

Approximate Floating Times

Hwy 10 Bridge — Hwy 89 Bridge: ⅓ day

Hwy 89 Bridge — Sheep Mountain Access: ⅓ day

Sheep Mountain Access — Springdale Bridge: Full day

Springdale Bridge — Grey Bear Access: Full day

Grey Bear Access — Big Timber: ⅔ day

Floatfishing is a top way to work this part of the river, but you must do it with your wits about you. There are long slow pools lulling you nearly to the point of boredom, which suddenly gather themselves up and rear back into heavy tail waves as they tumble into the next pool. These waves are avoidable, but you have to be ready for them to navigate safely by.

As in the case above Livingston, stick to the main channel — side channels often spawn irrigation dams.

It will also pay to scout out your pick-up point with an eye to the weight of your boat. Most accesses do not have an improved launching ramp. In these places, you'll probably need a four-wheel drive to tug a boat and trailer up out of the river, or you'll have to carry the boat up the bank, a distance of twelve feet on the average.

Small Streams of the Missouri Headwaters

The smaller tributaries of the major rivers in South-Central Montana are practically limitless in the opportunities they hold for trout fishermen. Without the recognition and attendant pressures that come to big names like the Madison, Missouri, and Yellowstone, they are loaded with fish and heavy with a sense of discovery and solitude.

True, the trout they give up are smaller than the fish that reside in big water, but what they lack in size, they more than make up for in numbers and spunk. Also, small streams do not mean small fish only. In the elusive "average" small stream, I've found that at least one trout in ten will be in the 15-inch/one pound category, and you will also find the occasional trophy fish in these waters.

How occasional, and what do I mean by trophy? At least once every year, and for the past ten years, I've pulled a trout over three pounds from a small stream. The biggest I ever caught from such water weighed four and a half pounds. But the Montana Fish and Game Department once shocked a seventeen pound female brown from a brushy small stream in the area!

No, I'm not going to say where. Although it may seem selfish at first, I don't plan to name any small stream specifically, even as an example of typical conditions. While there might be something gained by citing "Jones Creek" as a good example of a meadow stream, Jones Creek would end up the loser because of the pressure that would result from public identity.

Thus, rather than promoting a handful of possibilities — and destroying them in the process — let's proceed from the assumption that any watercourse more than two feet across, with occasional holes that are knee-deep or deeper, will hold trout. Just drive down any country road, and you will come across a small trout stream. Finding a place is just that simple, and charming.

For a complete listing of the names and locations of every small stream in the area **and** the size and kinds of fish they hold, refer to **The Montanans' Fishing Guide: East** (see "Maps and Source Materials in the Appendix of this book).

WHAT IS A SMALL STREAM?

For purposes of identification, let's define a small stream as "any watercourse that can be easily and frequently crossed, at typical summer levels, by an angler in hip waders." Like most catch-all definitions, however, this one is lacking in some precision. In fact, there are three distinct classes of small streams in South Central Montana: mountain streams, meadow streams, and spring creeks. And each of them has peculiar demands of tackle and technique.

They all have a few characteristics in common, however. They are intimate, easy to fish, and just plain relaxing.

They also tend to be more dependable, less subject to ups and downs, than our major rivers. If a rain rise, or a cold snap, or dog day heat puts a lid on the Madison or the Missouri, trout will still be biting on a small stream, and they will go at it all day long. Unlike big water, midday fishing is excellent on small streams because they have plenty of shade. Given those similarities, then, let's take a look at each type of stream.

MOUNTAIN STREAMS

Mountain streams are characterized by a steep-pitching bed, fast, frothy water, and a course that carries them down the bottom of a comparatively narrow canyon. They are relatively straight, studded with boulders, and usually located on public (National Forest) land.

Trout species commonly found in mountain streams are brook, cutthroat, rainbow, and occasionally grayling (grayling aren't really a trout, but they're close enough). The average fish runs eight to nine inches, 12-inchers are not unusual, but a 15-inch fish is exceptional.

Finding a mountain stream to fish involves nothing more than a drive up some logging road. Logging roads, common extensions of county roads, lead up into the mountains, and are open to the public, though you should be aware of two dangers: highballing logging trucks coming the other way and signs of road deterioration. When logging roads begin to turn into two-track ruts of muck and mire, they seldom get better ahead. If you have a conventional passenger vehicle, don't try to extend its limited rough-country capabilities — this could turn into a long walk out.

Once you're in a mountain stream environment, you're home free. You can fish anywhere you can walk to so long as you're on Forest Service ground, which means just about everywhere. That's one of the pleasures of fishing these streams. Exceedingly eager trout are another. I don't believe I have ever been skunked on a mountain stream, where the fish always seem to be hungry; #20 midge preferences and Harvard sophistication are not their strong suit.

As in most cases, however, mountain streams are not perfect in most anglers' eyes. They harbor the smallest of the small stream trout, because their fast currents eat up fish energy that would otherwise be transformed into pounds and inches. They are also difficult to fish, paved by slick boulders and unforgiving of the misstep or misplaced cast in their swiftness.

Otherwise, they are great fun. The same swiftness that keeps fish small injects them with a stamina you just don't find in trout taken from slower streams. The water is easy to read too. Any slow moving pocket is a good bet for a trout. The two-dimensional eddies that form behind emerged boulders are the most common lies, followed by bank eddies. These bank eddies may be created by sweepers (downed logs jutting into the water), point bars (points of rock or gravel that form quiet, rotating pools behind them), or by the cut banks that rise on the outside of sharp curves in the bed. You will also find a definite sorting of trout by size. The larger and deeper the pocket you are fishing, the larger the trout you will pull from that hole.

Whatever tackle you prefer, you'll get the best results fishing it upstream. The swiftness of the water elevates terminal tackle above feeding zones or tugs it out of quiet pockets when you try to work it downstream. Practical working distances are another consideration. The consequences of line drag in this fast, bubbly stuff dictates short, accurate, rapid casts, and if you don't approach trout from their back side, you'll spook them at such intimate ranges.

Mountain streams are at their best from mid-July through mid-September. Because of their elevation, in the fall they are the first streams to cool off, literally and figuratively. In the late spring they are wild with run-off, virtually unfishable, and downright dangerous, sometimes bearing a load of water 100 times their normal volume.

Mountain Stream Tackle

Fly fishermen will appreciate the virtues of a short 5- to 6-foot rod on a mountain stream. Casting distances are not great, but you will do a lot of it. Short rods are accurate and fast, and they don't tire you out. Incidentally, if you don't own a "flea" rod but have an ultra-light spinning rod with a movable reel seat, it just may do yeoman's duty as a short fly rod. Most ultra-light spinning rods have a parabolic action, the same action that defines a fly rod. As long as you can move a fly reel down to the end of the butt, your ultra-light spinning rod should do fine, and you'll save money in the bargain.

Floating fly line is the match for these small streams and small rods. You won't have to cast far or dredge deep holes to tempt a trout. You may benefit from a significantly heavier line than would seem normal. I prefer a 6-weight on these short rods because the moment of loading is easier to perceive.

Waders, or at least hip boots, are a virtual necessity. In order to work upstream with a fly you must get into position directly downstream of your target, and 95% of the time you'll have to wade to do this. Wet wading, even in midsummer, is out, unless you enjoy 45° footbaths. Mountain streams seldom rise above that temperature.

121

You should also carpet the soles of rubber-soled waders to get a better grip on slippery rocks under swift water. Use indoor/outdoor carpeting and a good contact cement. The brand of cement I've found best is called "Barge," and you can buy it at most cobbler shops.

There are no secrets of the most effective fly patterns in mountain streams. These mountain trout are willing to take anything. I've had great success on a Sofa Pillow, a huge dry fly that imitates the adult stage of a salmon fly, an insect that never hatches in these small streams! Mountain trout also seem to take a dry with as much gusto as a wet, streamer, or nymph, so owing to the special thrill of seeing these fish take it on top, I virtually always fish a dry. About the only condescension I make to patterns is that I like my flies bright and large so they're easy to see in the fast and bubbly water. #12 is the standard size, and the pattern to use is either a Royal Coachman, a Light Cahill, a Grasshopper, or a Goofus Bug.

Spinning with lures in mountain streams is a light tackle proposition. Like fly fishing, you'll get the best results fishing your hardware upstream, on short, snappy casts into quiet pockets. Trout are on the small side, so line in the 2- to 4-pound category equals a few of the odds, and handles the tiny, light lures you should use. The pockets and pools you'll be fishing won't be deep, and the water will be swift. A large, heavy lure sinks too quickly, and you'll have trouble gathering in line fast enough to set it to good action.

Instead, choose small spinners and spoons in silver and gold. #0 or #1 Mepps are standards, as are #4 Panther Martin spinners. "Flyweight" spoons like the Dardevle "Spinnie" and "Skeeter" are other regular producers.

Don't use snapswivels with this ultra-light equipment. When you're dealing with such small lures, swivels dampen the action and elongate a lure's appearance, cutting down on its attractiveness.

Baitfishing in small mountain streams is the most difficult technique of all. A small worm on a #8 hook, with a pinch of shot six inches from the bait, packs plenty of appeal for these trout, but controlling that bait under typical mountain stream conditions requires a master's touch. Bites are difficult to distinguish from the rap of bottom, and more often than not, your offering is rudely yanked out of a pocket by the current before a fish gets a chance to smell it out and size it up. Occasionally you can still-fish a cut bank effectively, but they aren't too common on mountain streams. When you find one, you usually have to sneak to the edge of the bank and drop your worm straight down, being acutely aware of bank vibrations set up by your feet, your shadow, and your silhouette. In general, if you are an excellent drift fisherman, you'll do well on a mountain stream. If you prefer to put a worm on a hook and wait, you'd be wiser to try elsewhere.

Whatever style of tackle you choose, know that trout from a mountain stream are a special gift in one respect. The cold, swift water makes them absolutely the best eating of any trout in Montana. If you enjoy eating fish, pan-fry a mess of 8- to 10-inchers over a campfire; then sit back and enjoy!

MEADOW STREAMS

Meadow streams generally begin at the transition zone where mountain conifers give way to cottonwood and aspen. Tight mountain canyons open up into valleys, the pitch of the stream bed becomes less severe, and the water gentles out, wandering around comfortable meanders in an endless succession of riffles and pools.

Meadow streams generally harbor brook and rainbow trout, and an occasional brown. Montana brookies don't get as big as these trout do in the East: a 12-incher is a good fish; a 16-incher exceptional. Brookies in this environment average an honest ten inches, rainbows twelve, with the rare lunker reaching two to three pounds.

Look for meadow streams on gentle-sloping valley highlands, below timberline and above the pancake-flat topography of true bottomlands. You can often spot them from afar by the thread of brush and trees that mark their banks, cutting through the sterile sameness of intensively-farmed lands and manicured pastures. I'm not sure why, but the back roads that lead to them usually cut them at right angles rather than following their path.

Meadow streams usually flow through private lands, so you'll have to get permission to fish them. It isn't hard to come by. Because so few anglers fish meadow streams in the West, landowners haven't been nuisanced into knee-jerk "no's." But before you go to the trouble of tracing down an owner, evaluate the general appearance of the stream.

"Modern" farming practices, specifically plowing every inch of tillable soil up to and including the front lawn, produce poor wildlife habitat. If the stream you're sizing up has an overall shallow look, with little or no shading vegetation along its banks and an unstable shore, indicated by a margin of pebbles and cobbles rather than well-defined, sharp banks, look elsewhere. It's likely that there are some trout in the stream, but it doesn't have the carrying potential of kinder water and bank conditions. On the other hand, if you find some inviting little glen, with lots of bankbrush or lush grasses bordering the stream, and an occasional deep hole introduced by a champagne riffle, you're likely to find superb fishing.

One other suggestion. If you get permission, and you probably will, jot down your benefactor's name and address and send him a note of thanks or a Christmas card with a few words of acknowledgment. It takes so little and it means so much to both of you, because you'll always be welcomed back.

Once you're on the stream, you'll find two places high in the numbers of trout they'll turn up: rotating eddies and bank eddies. Both conditions usually arise at a bend in the river bed — rotating eddies on the inside of the curve; bank eddies on the outside.

Rotating eddies usually lie downstream of a riffle or bar and amount to a slowly swirling pool of water that spins away from the main current, out toward the bank, and then back toward the riffle to rejoin the main current. Looking downriver, eddies on the right will turn clockwise and those on the left, counter-clockwise. Trout in meadows invariably station themselves along the "eddy fence," the loosely-defined dividing line between the main current and the slow water of the rotating eddy. In large, powerful rotating eddies, the reverse flow of water will create a cutbank along the shore. When they're present, look for trout there too.

Bank eddies will lie opposite or slightly below rotating eddies and are the result of currents swinging to the outside of the bend, where they carve deep holes in the bed and form steep cut-banks. Like rotating eddies, they will develop an eddy fence. Trout generally lie just inside that fence, where they watch the main current for food sweeping by.

Although I'd rate these two stations as the most likely ones in which to snare a trout in a meadow stream, they aren't the only lies. Pay close attention to any slow-moving (but not dead) water that appears to have some depth to it, especially when it occurs just below a shallow riffle. Riffles are a stream's food factory. Holes are places where trout can rest and hide. Whenever they occur side by side, there're sure to be trout in the picture as well.

Meadow Tackle and Techniques

Fly rods should be chosen with an eye to bank conditions. Some meadow streams are brushy and closed in, and if this is the case, you will do well to use the same short rod recommended for mountain streams. If banks are reasonably open, I call a 7½-foot 5 or 6 weight-rod an ideal match for meadow conditions.

Although the rare, very large rotating eddy may justify a sink-tip line, you'll find most conditions will be well covered with a floating line. As in mountain streams, accuracy is an important part of meadowland fishing, but casts need not be long; however, you will need the freedom of movement and approach afforded by waders.

Very clear water (you can see bottom at waist

depths) dictates working a fly upstream. Otherwise, I've had equal success working flies across
and downcurrent. The trout in these waters aren't
particularly leader-shy, so I tend to use short 7-foot
leaders with rather heavy tippets. If you have a lot
of brush to contend with, this practice will save a
lot of flies that would otherwise end up in the trees.

Recommended fly patterns again begin with
dries. More often than not, meadowland trout will
succumb to a dry, and so long as that possibility
exists, I prefer to fish on top. Usually, these trout
will fall for a Royal Coachman when no hatch is
evident. If that doesn't work, try an imitation of a
terrestrial: a hopper, an ant, or a beetle. Remember that these fish are bank-oriented due to
the proportionately large food contribution made
by the land to the stream.

Should there be a hatch, I feel confident in say-
ing that you can match it to a trout's satisfaction
with either a Light Cahill or a Blue Dun on an #14
hook. Adams, Mosquito, Quill Gordon, and Dark
Hendrickson are other patterns the trout seem to
like.

If trout refuse you on top, try a Gold Ribbed
Hare's Ear nymph, a perennial favorite in these
waters. Other nymph patterns that have proved
attractive include the Mites and the Muskrat Caddis.

Meadowland streams are fertile places to plumb
with a wet fly — more so than in any other waters
in the area, though I don't know why. Fish either a
Coachman, a Leadwing Coachman, or a Dark
Hendrickson downcurent for the greatest appeal.
I've had the least luck on streamers in meadow-
lands, probably because I perceive these streams
as "fly" water and reserve streamer fishing for

major rivers. In any event, a #10 Muddler Minnow will be all that you'll need.

Spinning with lures calls for the same tackle and techniques that work best in mountain streams: ultra-light rods and reels, 2- to 4-pound test line, and light $\frac{1}{16}$- to $\frac{1}{8}$-ounce lures. The only difference results from the slower currents common to a meadow stream. You can make longer casts, and you may need an additional pinch of split shot above the lure to get down to the deeper feeding zones. I also prefer to work a lure up-or-cross-current. This approach also gets your hardware down to where the action is.

Baitfishing in these waters is superb; worms and meadow creeks were made for each other, especially when the water is cloudy or muddy with rain or spring run-off. Use enough lead to get you down to the bottom, but not so much that you are anchored there. Bait up with a large angle worm or half a nightcrawler (more meat than this usually results in half-biters) and drift it along the eddy fences. When the water's cloudy, you needn't make long casts. In fact, you'll take a lot of trout right off your rod tip. Another place that's virtually guaranteed for a bite lies at the confluence of the reverse flow from a rotating eddy with the main current.

Baitfishing in these waters is superb; worms and meadow creeks were made for each other, especially when the water is cloudy or muddy with rain or spring run-off. Use enough lead to get you down to the bottom, but not so much that you are anchored there. Bait up with a large angle worm or half a nightcrawler (more meat than this usually results in half-biters) and drift it along the eddy fences. When the water's cloudy, you needn't make

TOP FLIES

If I had to winnow out a barebones selection of flies from the hundreds of patterns that work, not just on small streams, but throughout the Missouri Headwaters, they would be:

Dries — #14 Royal Wulff, #14 Adams, #14 Elk Hair Caddis

Nymphs — #8 Green Wooly Worm, #8 Brown Wooly Worm, #8 Montana Nymph

Streamers — #6 Muddler, #Spruce, #6 Royal Coachman

long casts. In fact, you'll take a lot of trout right off your rod tip. Another place that's virtually guaranteed for a bite lies at the confluence of the reverse flow from a rotating eddy with the main current. Since bait-fishing is usually successful in meadow streams, I recommend this kind of fishing for those who have yet to take their first trout — perhaps your wife, children, or friends.

SPRING CREEKS

As their name implies, spring creeks generally originate from springs welling up from the ground. These creeks are usually found winding their way across the flattest, lowest ground in the major river valleys.

Some spring creeks are short, bubbling up within casting distance of a major river. Others run for miles, often paralleling a larger water-course. Whatever their length, they're usually loaded with brown trout that average twelve inches with an occasional monster up to six or seven pounds. Rainbows and brookies may also turn up on your hook, but they are in a distinct minority.

Spring creeks are prone to excessive meandering, and usually they wander through lush bottom-lands devoid of bank brush. Their bed contours are uniform, and so is temperature, which frequently results in aquatic vegetation, commonly duckweek or watercress.

Their nature and origin suggest several ideas about spring creeks and the kind of fishing they offer. They are seldom affected by rain-rises or run-off, cold snaps or heat waves. Of all the small streams, they are generally the most fertile and hold the largest fish. Because of their aquatic vegetation, they are difficult to fish with spinning tackle or sinking flies. For this reason, and because of the absence of bank growth, spring creeks are a Shangri-la for the dry fly fisherman.

Like meadow streams, spring creeks invariably flow through private lands, and getting permission to fish them can be difficult. Because they are so ideally suited to dry fly fishing, some of them are jealously guarded by landowners. Others are leased to individuals, or you are charged a rod fee to fish. Those that do have some public availability are heavily pressured by sophisticated trout fishermen.

Still, if you are addicted to the dry fly, the effort to fish these streams will have ample reward. Their slow currents, flat waters, casting room, and sleek, perfectly-conditioned trout are as close to paradise as you'll find.

The best fishing in spring creeks lies in two places: against banks, and in the current lanes and boils that form around clogs of weeds. Because of the even bed contours, stations that are common to swifter streams — like rotating eddies, bank eddies, two-dimensional eddies and riffle tails — don't exist in spring creeks.

Instead, trout position themselves under the cutbanks that occur on the outside of each meander, and in pockets in the duckweed and watercress that face out into clear channels. Current boils that burp up immediately behind flats of weeds are another favorite lie.

The most practical way to fish all these lies is into the current. Wade up the middle of the creek, batting away at banks, boils, and channels. The deeper and darker the water you cast to, the more likely it is to harbor a fish.

Spring Creek Tackle

Fly fishing is easiest with a 7- to 8-foot 6-weight rod. Spring creeks are almost always clear, so you'll need some reach to stay hidden from the fish.

Long fragile leaders are in order too — 5X or 6X tippets on at least nine feet of leader. This is also one of the few situations where I recommend leader sink, especialy on a bright sunny day. Even hairlines cast a shadow like a hawser on calm, clear water.

Those gossamer leaders also dictate a landing net, though I always carry one whenever I'm fishing. To trout that you want to release, a net is kinder than beaching.

Although spring creek trout can be incredibly selective about what they'll take, don't confront this thorny problem unless you have to. Because of the pasture environment, a great number of terrestrials tumble into the water, so even though the fish may be rising to pinhead midges, you can often get them to respond to a grasshopper, ant, spider, beetle, or similar creeping nightmare. I always start with a grasshopper imitation, a big fly easy to fish and easy to see. Here's another trick to consider — try fishing a Muddler Minnow dry. Muddlers are a close match to a type of grasshopper that locals call a "clacker" and that trout seem to favor over the more common redleg grasshopper. Goofus Bugs, Humpies and Irrestibles are other patterns you should have with you.

If trout turn these offerings down flat, well, you might then entertain the madness of matching the hatch and fishing miniscule flies, but first try one more wild guess — a mosquito. Spring creek bottoms are loaded with them, suggesting something else not to be without: insect repellent.

Spinfishing in many spring creeks is practically impossible because of weeds. If you can find open water, use ultra light rods and reels, light line, and small lures. One other problem you'll face, however, is getting reach out of small, light lures. As in fly fishing, distance between you and your quarry is central to getting strikes, but the heavy lures that would give you distance sink to the bottom unless retrieved just this side of the speed of light.

Baitfishing presents similar complications. You can snake an occasional trout from under a cutbank by floating a live grasshopper downstream, and in open water, drift-fishing an unweighted worm may take fish. But for the most part, you will be wise to stick to mountain and meadow streams if you're a spin fisherman, leaving spring creeks to the feather merchants.

Lakes of South-Central Montana

Although the area isn't noted for them, South-Central Montana is blessed with an abundance of lakes. Not only are their numbers great, their shorelines, the fish they harbor, and the fishing styles they lend themselves to define the meaning of diversity.

Some lakes are tiny emeralds set at the base of alpine peaks. Others sparkle like bright diamonds gracing the finger-like tributaries of larger streams. If big water is more to your liking, great reservoirs adorn the arms of our mightiest rivers.

The lake surroundings are as varied as their size: sere alpine meadows, thick stands of pine and fir, and the rolling sagebrush hills of the High Plains. What's more, the fish you can catch in these lakes are as exciting as the scenery. Depending on the lake where you wet your line, you can tempt native cutthroat trout, grayling, rainbow, brookies, browns, lake trout, and even rare golden trout!

From an angling point of view, however, lake opportunities can be whittled down to two categories: alpine lakes and lowland lakes. The class of lake you're fishing determines the most likely approach.

ALPINE LAKES: TAKE YOUR PICK

Alpine lakes are glacial in origin, and they lie above 6,000 feet. You can seldom reach them via the family car, but about half the alpine lakes in the area are accessible to some form of off-road transportation: a four-wheel drive vehicle, a trail bike, or an ATV. The other half are limited, either by obstacles or by the law, to foot or horseback access.

Lakes of the Missouri Headwaters

For a complete listing of the names and locations of alpine lakes in the Missouri Headwaters, refer to **The Montanans' Fishing Guide: East**. (See "Maps and Source Materials" in the Appendix of this book).

There are over 500 alpine lakes in the mountains of South-central Montana, and every one of them is nestled in spectacular scenery. It would be pointless and unnecessary to discuss each lake as a separate entity, because they all march to the same drummer.

Fishing them is essentially a mid-summer pursuit, roughly from July 1 until the middle of September. Before and after this time, they're either covered with ice, or the trails that lead into them are blocked by snow drifts. If you are familiar with the area and with the relative lateness or early arrival of spring or fall, you can often ignore this rule and find fishing two weeks earlier or later. But if you're a visitor, do some careful checking with game wardens or forestry personnel before attempting to hike into a high mountain lake in June or late September.

Picking a place to fish is largely a matter of map study and/or field research. I would do a disservice to your sport and yourself by recommending a specific place to go — it would only concentrate fishing pressure there. One of the greatest gifts of fishing in the high country is the sense of solitude that pervades the experience, and Lord knows, there are enough lakes to go around.

You can come up with a dozen possibilities on your own across the counter of any tackle shop, and twenty more through the signs you'll see during an hour's drive through National Forest lands. Ranger stations and district fish and game headquarters are another source of information, and these places also have maps for sale or as a giveaway. However, if you can't find accurate, first-hand thorough information about a lake you plan to fish, buy a topographical map of the area, available in most tackle shops, and study it carefully with an eye to the existence and condition of any trails in to your lake, to the distance in, and to the elevation gained in hiking in. If you're new to this game, and afoot, think twice if you'll be gaining an average of more than 200 feet of elevation per mile of trail, or if you'll be covering more than six miles in a day. It's been my experience that these figures define the upper limits of the comfortable middle ground for a beginning mountain hiker.

Topo maps also reveal lake clusters. Often a particular lake will have between three and six sister lakes within a mile radius. Knowing their existence and location is one of the tricks to catching trout in the high country. When fish in one lake are turned off, they can be red hot in sister lake a quarter mile away, so you throw some important odds in your favor when you choose a destination with more than one place to fish.

You should also be aware of a malady unique to high elevation lakes, the phenomenon known as "freezing out." During especially hard winters, the trout population in an alpine lake can be wiped out. It is not a matter of the lake's turning into one collossal ice cube, but rather of oxygen deprivation. Rotting vegetation from the summer consumes all the oxygen in the water, and there is no fresh supply because of the cap of solid ice. Lakes that freeze out usually have extensive shallows and vegetation. When you note that condition, and no sign of trout or fry, there's a strong possibility the lake has been frozen out.

SPECIAL EQUIPMENT FOR MOUNTAIN LAKES

Because your capacity to tote tackle will be limited, you should consider investing in some specialized equipment. "Pack" or "trail" rods break down into four or five sections and fit into an 18- to 24-inch carrying case. They come as fly rods or spinning rods or combination spinning/fly rods. It's this latter combination I recommend and prefer since it gives the latitude to match all feeding patterns in one compact package.

Consider taking a fly reel with two arbors. Load one with weight-forward floating line and the other with weight-forward sinking line. If you really want to conserve space and weight, splice half a floating line to half a sinking line back-to-back. As the need for either arises, you just unspool and reverse the line.

For spinning with lures or bait, take a small ultra-light reel loaded with a 2- or 4-pound test line. Mountain trout are shy, and this weight line will handle the light lures they prefer.

Chest waders afford a substantial advantage in that they often give the twenty feet of extra reach needed to cast beyond muddy shallows. However, consider investing in special lightweight, stocking-foot waders. Conventional boots will add between six and fifteen pounds to the weight you must carry up the mountain. For quality and durability, Red Ball's "Flyweights" are the lightweights I prefer.

Carry this equipment, and your fly or spinning terminal tackle, in a "day pack," a small backpack that distributes the load across the shoulders and back and leaves both the hands free. There will also be enough room left for lunch.

One item not to pack in is an inflatable boat. Speaking as one who has lugged what seemed like a half-ton of rubber up more trails than I care to remember, they're not worth the effort. You'll find that if you can't catch trout from the shore, they won't be any more cooperative in the middle of the lake.

FINDING FISH IN AN ALPINE LAKE

The most likely spot to find feeding trout is at the lake's inlet. Most alpine lakes have an inlet stream, though many of these brooklets flow under a cover of scree or talus. If you don't see running water, circle the lake and listen or water beneath rock slides.

Outlet streams are the second place to look. The problem here is that outlets are often at the shallowest part of a lake, and trout are most likely to feed near the margins of shallow water, where it plummets into deep, dark water. If you can't reach a drop-off with your cast, fish the closest drop-off to the outlet that you can reach.

Banks and subsurface structures that pitch down sharply from shore are the third most likely place for trout to congregate. Look for these places at the foot of cliffs and below talus slopes.

Although you'd think that fish who don't see blue sky or a decent meal for nine months out of the year would swim up into wet grass for the chance to take your hook, mountain trout can be maddeningly selective in their feeding times and habits. Rather than having prolonged and consistent feeding periods, these fish tend to turn on and off with the suddenness and unpredictability of a summer thunderstorm. A lake can be flat calm without a rise for half a day and then suddenly boil with activity for no apparent reason.

Keep this in mind, should your initial efforts prove fruitless, and keep in mind the sister lakes that may lie over the hill. Alpine lakes are responsive to the same techniques, but they are unique in terms of feeding periods. Still, you'll find, as a loose rule of thumb, that they are most likely to come alive between two and five in the afternoon; therefore plan to stick to your fishing during this period.

FISHING WITH FLIES, LURES, AND BAIT

Fly fishing is a matter of long casts, long light leaders, and small flies. Alpine lakes are clear, and the fish in them wary. Long casts put distance and cover between you and your quarry, and they also allow you to reach the drop-offs at the edge of shallows. These drop-offs are usually the most productive places to fish with a fly because shallow water acts as an insect incubator, and trout cruise the shallows in search of insects.

Although you will probably see many rises, you'll find it difficult to take a mountain trout on a dry, though I cannot say why. As a rule, when trout are rising, they want a nymph or wet fly fished just under the surface film and retrieved fast enough to make a little wake. If trout are not rising, fish a small weighted nymph deep, off the edge of drop-offs, and retrieve it in long, slow strips of line that cause the fly to rise and fall in gentle rhythms, like a slow-motion jig.

If you know grayling to be in the lake you're fishing, lead off with a #14 wet fly, gray in color. A Hare's Ear is one pattern that's often successful. Whether they're feeding on top or below the surface, grayling can't turn down a gray fly. Generally, a #14 fly is the largest pattern you should pack in to a mountain lake. You will probably have the best luck with #16 and #18 hooks, and there will be an occasional need for #20 patterns.

Spinfishing also requires a tiny pursuit. Use ¼-ounce-and-under spoons and spinners. Lures that produce a lot of action at the slowest speeds will catch the most fish. To get some extra reach, pinch a split shot six inches ahead of your lure. The shot also helps get the lure down deep, and mountain trout usually prefer a deep presentation. Unless you experience unmanageable line kink, don't use snapswivels. They dampen the action of these small lures and increase their apparent size, to the detriment of their overall appeal.

If you are a spinfisherman exclusively and unfamiliar with the use of a fly rod, take a clear plastic casting bubble so you can fish flies with your spinning rod. Trout in mountain lakes exhibit a decided preference for flies, and you'll be hobbling yourself if you're limited to lures alone.

You can also fish wet flies or nymphs with the bubble. The technique is nothing more than a slow retrieve and stop — slow retrieve and stop — so the

Flies
Adams
Elk Hair Caddis
Wooly Worm
Hare's Ear
Mosquito

Lures
Panther Martin
Mepps
Roostertail
Thomas Cyclone
Goldfish

fly rides up and then sinks. Strike as soon as the bubble dips. Trout don't hold on to flies the way they will to a bait.

You'll find baitfishing the least productive in a mountain lake. It will catch fish, but not on a par with flies or lures, so it's a technique I usually reserve for those slack periods when nothing else seems to work, in the slim hope of an accidental meeting between worm and trout.

Of all the possible baits, small garden worms will work the best. Fish them three to four feet beneath a float, right at the edge of drop-offs. If you know the species of trout that inhabit individual lakes, pick a place with rainbows or brookies. They seem to like worms more than cutthroats, goldens, or grayling.

LOWLAND LAKES: BIG WATER — BIG TROUT

Roughly half the lowland lakes in South Central Montana are man-made. They are impoundments created to store water for irrigation, to control flooding, and to generate power. The other half are natural. Both have a great deal in common, however, in that they are much larger bodies of water than alpine lakes, and legally and practically, most of them can be fished all year long. In addition, they are all accessible to conventional transportation, including trailered boats.

Brown and rainbow trout are in the majority in these bodies of water, but a few have populations of cutthroat and grayling. Because of longer open-water periods (which equals a longer growing season), a more than ample food supply, and the relaxed atmosphere of still waters, trout in lowland lakes put on pounds. They are, on the average, larger fish than their stream or river-dwelling brethren, and when a catch makes the record books, it invariably comes from one of these lakes.

Other than standard trout tackle, two pieces of equipment will prove their worth on a lake: a boat and an electronic depth sounder. A boat, and by that term I mean any floating device including an inflatable caster's tube, will enable you to reach channels, drop-offs, and shorelines that are beyond the range of a man afoot. Depth sounders are reputed to be "fish finders," but that's not their real value. They reveal the bottom structure of a lake, in turn providing valuable clues to the whereabouts of fish.

In general, these hotspots fall into four categories.

• Lake inlets. Any stream, river, or freshet entering a lake will be attractive to trout. Such water funnels food into the lake, it boosts oxygen levels around the immediate area, and it cools warmish lake waters in the summer. In natural lakes, lake outlets are attractive, essentially for the same reason. This is not true of most man-made lakes because the shore structure around a dam plummets to the bottom without any attractive shoaling or shelving.

• Shoals, bars or submerged cliffs that border deep water. The shallow water acts as a food factory, and the deep water affords cruising fish protection and temperatures to their liking.

• Submerged channels. In every man-made lake, the old river bed that is now flooded will still carry a current that moves from inlet to outlet. Trout will station themselves in or above this channel in response to the extra food and oxygen the current carries. Natural lakes will incorporate similar current lanes, but they are difficult to identify because bottom structure has a more subtle influence on their meanderings.

• Large points and islands. These formations create current swirls by acting as obstacles to current lanes, or to wind-driven currents. The troubled water increases oxygen levels, moderates temperatures, and fosters smaller aquatic life, which in turn attracts trout.

TACKLE AND TECHNIQUES

Fly fishing in lowland lakes is especially good around inlet streams and weedy shallows. The ability to cast long distances counts, so use weight-forward tapers and 8- or 9-foot rods. Large nymphs, from #10 to #6 produce best, followed by high floating dry flies from #16 to #12.

If you are fishing in more than twenty feet of water, a sinking line is in order. When fishing with nymphs, try a variety of retrieves, from slow and measured to fast and jerky. One day the trout want it one way — the next day they expect a different performance. Even when the trout are rising, you'll catch more on a nymph than a dry. If you prefer to fish dry, the trick is to watch a rising trout with an eye to the direction he's headed. Drop the fly well ahead of him and wait until you're sure he's passed by before you mend your line. This can take five minutes or more, but be patient. You are more likely to take a trophy trout fishing in a lake than in a river, so patience has its reward.

Spinfishing with lures, from a purely practical

Flies
Irresistible
Goofus Bug
Wooley Worm
Bitch Creek
Girdle Bug
Lures
Krocodile
Panther Martin
Thomas Cyclone
Wonderlure
Little Jewel

point of view, is a matter of shorecasting. If you have a boat, you'll catch as many if not more fish by trolling, and with less effort. Concentrate on covering the water around lake inlets, large points, and steep drop-offs close to shore. As in fly fishing, distance counts, so I recommend that you put together a rig capable of long casts. My favorite lake casting outfit is a 7½-foot light action parabolic rod with outsized guides and an ultra-light reel loaded to the lip with 4-pound test. This combination is capable of lobbing a ½-ounce spoon up to fifty yards, and it's that kind of reach that will take the most trout. Most lake casting situations will be satisfied by a spoon or a sinking minnow plug. A slow retrieve that barely sets the lure to motion is usually best because it keeps the lure hugging bottom, and as long as trout aren't actively rising, that's where they'll usually be. If fish are rising, it will also pay to have a clear plastic casting bubble and a selection of flies. There are times when trout in lakes want insects only, and if you aren't familiar with conventional fly fishing, the fly-bubble technique is the only way you'll be able to take fish.

Baitfishing in lakes is usually best in the spring and fall. The colder water temperatures at this time lure trout close to the surface and in toward shore, and because there are relatively few insects around, fish will take a bait with no questions asked; furthermore, midsummer fishing with most baits usually finds trash fish beating trout to your hook.

The best bait and rigging, whatever the time of year, is a worm on a snelled hook, twelve inches above a bell sinker. Skewer a small marshmallow on the hook along with the worm. It will float the bait up off the bottom, where it is easier for trout to see and harder for trash fish like suckers to get. You can also "blow" a worm, by injecting it with air, so it floats by itself. Fishing a worm beneath a float is another possibility when trout are in shallow water. Leave enough line between float and bait so the bait can be seen from the bottom. Other baits that may prove attractive include corn, cheese, sucker meat, cured roe, salmon eggs, and live sculpin.

The best place to baitfish in a lake is at the edge of a drop-off. If that drop-off rests next to some sort of current lane or swirl, so much the better.

Trolling is a top tactic for trout in area lakes, and especially attractive in that once you figure out where the fish are and what they're taking, you can put a rod in anyone's hand and he will catch fish. Trolling is one time when a depth finder is doubly handy, because it reveals the depth and the level the trout are at. According to water temperatures, trout may be found anywhere from ten feet below the surface in the spring to fifty feet below in midsummer. A finder will spell out the thermocline they're in at the moment.

Once you know where the fish are, the only task left is to put together a combination of line and terminal tackle that will get down to the level of the trout. Here are some hints about how to do this:

Light line will troll any given lure deeper than heavy line because it offers less resistance in the water.

Adding a keel sinker the same weight as the lure you're using will double your trolling depth.

Metered line, which changes color at ten foot intervals, is the only reliable way to troll a lure at the same depth every time.

Spinners troll closest to the surface, spoons troll

Montana Trout Are Naturals

Montana's trout stocking program is limited. With the exception of fingerlings used to bolster lakes within sufficient spawning opportunities for their carrying capacity, nature provides for replenishment of trout. This policy is the result of studies which have indicated that the practice of stocking trout can actually cause a fishery to deteriorate in quality, in vigor, and even in carrying capacity.

mid-ranges, and lipped plugs troll the deepest.

In mid-summer, when trout are at their lowest levels, you may have to use leadcore or wire line, or planers, to get down to the fish.

Once you establish the level at which trout are working, follow that depth contour along the shoreline. For every fish in the middle of the lake, there will be four close to shore. If you do not have a depth finder, you can still determine the level at which trout are feeding, by trolling at different depths. Surface temperatures of the water provides another good lead. If it is below seventy degrees, trout will probably suspend above 20-foot depths. If the surface lake waters are higher than seventy degrees, trout will be feeding in twenty feet of water or more.

LAKE DIRECTORY

Canyon Ferry Reservoir is the first major impoundment on the Missouri River. It's located east of Helena and is accessible on the west shore from US 12. Montana 284 affords access from the east.

The lake is twenty-five miles long and averages three miles wide. The best trolling is usually within a hundred yards of shore, around rocky points and steep drop-offs. Shorecasters and bait-fishermen also prosper in these places, and in the small bays at the mouths of creeks.

Canyon Ferry is best in the spring and fall, but fly fishermen often do well in mid-summer where the Missouri enters the lake, and around the mouths of small creeks.

There are many recreation areas, public campgrounds, and road accesses to the lake, and most of them have launching ramps.

Clark Canyon Reservoir (or Hap Hawkins Reservoir) lies south of Dillon on I-15. It has long enjoyed a reputation of trophy trout water, and football-fat rainbows and browns in the 2- to 4-pound category are common.

The best fly fishing is around the mouth of Red Rock River and Horse Prairie Creek. The best trolling and shore fishing is around the rock islands toward the dam, and off steep rocky points.

The reservoir has public campgrounds and launching ramps, and it is heavily fished all season long. Morning and evening are the best times for casting a lure or a fly, and trolling seems most productive when there is a wind-riffle on the water.

Cliff Lake is located southwest of the junction of US 287 with Montana 87, near the earthquake area. A good gravel road, approximately three miles north of the junction and plainly marked, leads to the lake.

Cliff lake is glacial in origin, and part of the chain bracketed by Elk Lake to the south and Wade Lake to the north. There is a public campground on the north end of the lake, and tourist camps along the east shore.

Rainbows predominate here, plus a few browns. Fish for them where white marly shallows drop off into deep blue-green water. You'll often see trout cruising these shallows, and you can stalk them like bonefish on tidal flats.

Although Cliff Lake has the reputation of having the poorest fishing in the lake chain, it is attractive in that it receives the lightest fishing pressure and camper-use.

Daily Lake is thirty miles north of Livingston, at the end of a 5½-mile gravel road, east of US 89. It has about a ¼-square-mile of surface and is relatively shallow.

The best fishing is at the deeper north end of the lake, whether you're trolling, or casting a lure or fly.

Daily Lake offers fair fishing for rainbow trout. There are also perch, walleye, and a few kokanee salmon there, as well as lots of swimmers and water skiers in the summer.

Elk Lake is situated at the head of Centennial Valley. To get to it, you must dip down into Idaho. After crossing Reynolds Pass on Montana 87, take the dirt road on the right, which follows the northern shoreline of Henry's Lake. Bear right as you leave the lake, and go up over Red Rock Pass. Bear right again at the fork above Upper Red Rock Lake, and follow the Elk Creek Road to the lake.

Be forewarned that this is not an all-weather road, so inquire about the conditions ahead, after a heavy rain or early or late in the season. Nor is it recommended for trailering large boats. If you're dead set on getting into Elk Lake at less than ideal times, an all-weather road leads to it from the town of Monida, but it's a long and bouncy ride.

Elk Lake has a real grab bag of fish: lake trout, rainbow, cutthroat, brookies, browns, and grayling. Trolling is generally best along the steep shores of the south end of the lake. Fly fishing is most productive at the shallow north end. Although most of the lake is accessible by foot, the trails are steep and rocky. You will do well to use a cartopper or a belly boat here. There is a tourist camp and public campground on the south end of the lake.

Lake Fishing for Warm Water Species

The headwaters of the Missouri are trout country, but if you're looking for a change of pace, there are largemouth bass in the oxbow ponds on the north side of the Jefferson River between Sappington Bridge and the Three Forks Bridge.

Daily Lake, thirty miles south of Livingston, was stocked with walleye catchables in 1979.

Hauser Lake is the second impoundment along the Missouri River, with waters that back right up to the foot of Canyon Ferry Dam. Access points are at Canyon Ferry Dam, and from Montana 453 north of Helena.

There are public campgrounds along the lakeshore, as well as tourist facilities. Fishing is for rainbows and a few browns. In general, this is a troller's lake, with the best action found along rocky, steep shores.

Hebgen Lake lies northwest of West Yellowstone. It's an impoundment along the Madison River and is most readily accessible from US 287, which follows the lake shore.

Trolling and shore fishing for browns and rainbows are best from the dam to the confluence of the north and south arms of the lake. The majority of fish are taken within two hundred yards of shore there. Fly-fishing is best near the mouths of the Madison River, Duck Creek, and the South Fork of the Madison. Some trophy-class trout are taken on flies from Hebgen in the middle of summer days, when the lake is calm.

There are both public and private camping, tourist, and boating facilities on the shores of Hebgen. Because of its proximity to Yellowstone Park, it gets heavily fished in July and August.

Hidden Lake lies two and a half miles north of Elk Lake. It's accessible by road, but it's a four-wheel drive proposition in all but perfect, dry weather. Follow the Elk Lake Road two and a half miles past the lake.

Hidden Lake has good fishing for rainbows, cutthroat, and rainbow/cutthroat crossbreeds. Because of steep brushy banks, fishing from shore is limited.

There is a boat livery and tourist camp on the north end of the lake, and unimproved campgrounds along the west shore.

Although access is relatively difficult, Hidden Lake takes a surprising amount of fishing pressure. I've also found the trout there to be unusually cooperative, but debatable table fare in the summer months. They develop a minty, mossy taste identical to that of Madison River fish.

Hyalite Lake is a modest-sized irrigation reservoir high in the mountains south of Bozeman. To get there, follow South 19th Street to the end of the pavement and turn left, up Hyalite Canyon.

Hyalite has good access from the dam, all along the east shore, with plenty of improved public campgrounds. The lake is too small for large boats, but it's a perfect lake for a cartopper.

Fishing there is for cutthroat and grayling, and for a rare brookie or rainbow. Fly fishing is best near lake tributaries; trolling and bait and spin-fishing are best close to the dam face and steep drop-offs.

Hyalite is a spring/fall lake, subject to an algae bloom in mid-summer. If you fish there in the warmer months, go deep, where the fish will be.

Lake Helena is a large bay or "arm" of Hauser Lake (see page 148).

Lima Reservoir is south of Dillon, on Red Rock River. Turn east at Lima, on I-15.

As a matter of fact, don't turn there. Because of extreme summer draw-downs, Lima Reservoir has poor fishing, so I'm told; so bad that I've been discouraged from trying it myself.

You may try Lima Reservoir and find the water

paved with finning trout, the bad report a clever lie; in this case, perpetuate the myth and consider your success initiative's reward.

Meadow Lake is a shallow impoundment along the Madison River north of Ennis. The north and east shores have good access; turn east at the tiny town of McAllister, on Montana 287.

This lake measures three and a half by three and a half miles, but it is not a "big boat" lake. The shallow, upper third of the reservoir lacks sufficient draft for even light motors, and there are limited trolling opportunities because of extensive beds of aquatic vegetation. This same salad complicates fly and lure casting from a boat. The only workable tactic is to cast between the weed beds. If you can keep your hooks clear, there are some nice browns and rainbows here.

The best time to fish Meadow Lake is after high water. It is so shallow that it gets as muddy as the Madison during run-off.

Otter/Goose Lakes lie between Hidden Lake and Cliff Lake. Access is by foot; take the trail that leads past Hidden Lake, or motor across Cliff Lake to the end of Horn Arm, then walk two miles up Lost Mine Canyon. It's a flat, easy trail.

The lakes lie only one eighth of a mile apart, and each is about ten acres in size. Their shorelines are shallow and snaggy, but these lakes hold some trophy-class rainbows and rainbow-cutthroat hybrids.

Flies are the most effective lure here, and the fish can be darned selective to boot. A trip in is an easy overnighter for a backpacker; fishing is usually best early in the morning and late in the evening.

Quake Lake lies downstream of Hebgen Dam, along US 287. It is a "natural" lake in that it was created by natural forces — by a huge landslide triggered by the earthquake of '59; otherwise, it is more akin to man-made lakes.

Fly and spin-casting from a light boat are the two most workable techniques on Quake Lake. The countless trees that were submerged when the waters rose eat trolled lures with a ravenous appetite, and they also take a substantial toll of cast lures.

As luck will have it, that's where the browns and rainbows like to hide — among the snags and stick-ups.

Red Rock Lakes lie at the foot of Red Rock Pass. They are closed to fishing. The area is a wildlife refuge, and the fishing closure protects nesting wildflowl.

Ruby Reserovir is an irrigation impoundment along the Ruby River, seven miles west of Alder, on a paved highway. The lake has a surface area of between three and four square miles, depending on the drawdown.

The eastern shore has free public access (BLM land), a boat ramp, and spare camping facilities. The best fishing is around the face of the dam, and off the rock outcrops on the east and west shore.

The mouth of the Ruby River is also good fishing when the lake is on the rise, but when it is falling, the current dirties the upper end of the lake, spoiling the fishing.

Dawn and dusk are the most reliable times to fish from shore because trout cruise along the shore at these times. If you have a boat, large rainbows go on the rise between nine and eleven a.m. in the middle of the lake, and they can be taken with flies or a cast lure. Trolling is best after ten, especially when there is a riffle on the water.

Wade Lake lies north of Cliff Lake, and it's accessible by the same road that takes you to Cliff.

Wade is the most popular lake in the chain because of its reputation as a trophy-trout lake. Several record rainbows and browns have been caught here.

As with Cliff Lake, you'll find the best fishing near marly shallows that drop off into deep water, and along steep banks. Shore fishing is limited at Wade, because of the steep banks, so a boat is recommended.

There is a public campground and tourist camp, with a boat livery, on the south end of the lake.

Willow Creek Reservoir is a small irrigation reservoir two miles east of the town of Harrison, which lies along US 287.

The best trolling is along the northeast shore of the lake and in the canyon near the dam. The area at the mouth of Willow Creek is one of the better shore fishing spots, and so are the mouths of Norwegian and Dry Hollow Creeks.

If you're a fly fisherman, try the shallow upper end of the reservoir in a belly-boat or a car-topper. Large rainbows and browns regularly prowl these flats in search of insects.

Salmon in the Missouri Headwaters

...Well, sort of. A dozen years ago, coho salmon were introduced to several lowland reservoirs in the area; and earlier, kokanee (or landlocked sockeye). Salmon were transplanted from across the Continentel Divide. Neither species met with marked success, though trollers occasionally pick up a relic of the original transplant population.

Appendix

Fish of the
Missouri Headwaters

BROOK TROUT
Salvelinus fontinalis

(Local name: Native)

Brook trout are easily and positively identified by side coloring, red spots surrounded by halos of blue. Vermiculations — these look like worm trails — on their olive-to-greenish brown back are another characteristic unique to the species.

Brookies are found in virtually every tributary of the Missouri and in many lakes. They prefer moderate flow velocities, however, so you usually catch them from small side channels and backwaters of the larger, swifter rivers.

Brook trout up to nine pounds have been recorded in Montana, but a fish of such proportions is a rarity indeed. A good brookie in the Missouri drainage is 12- to 13-inches.

Harvard sophistication has never been the brookies' strong suit. They will take about any bait, fly, or lure when they are in a feeding mood. In late summer and fall, the mating colors on large males will take your breath away.

Being able to positively identify a brook trout is important, because you may keep a separate limit of brookies over and above the limit on our coldwater sportfish. Being a lover of trout flesh, I find this comforting indeed. There is no better eating than a mess of pan-sized brookies, fried over a campfire. When they are around, I throw other trout back, keeping the brookies for the pan.

Brook trout are not really a trout — they're a char. Their closest

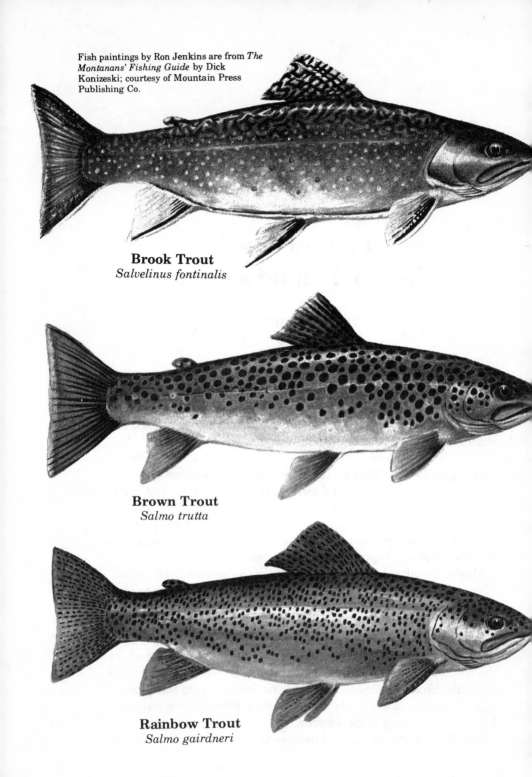

Fish paintings by Ron Jenkins are from *The Montanans' Fishing Guide* by Dick Konizeski; courtesy of Mountain Press Publishing Co.

Brook Trout
Salvelinus fontinalis

Brown Trout
Salmo trutta

Rainbow Trout
Salmo gairdneri

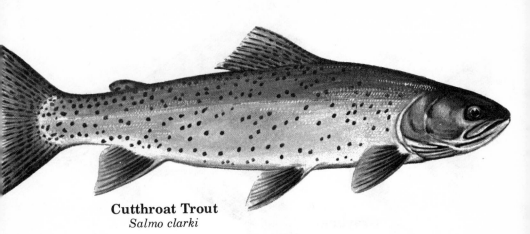

Cutthroat Trout
Salmo clarki

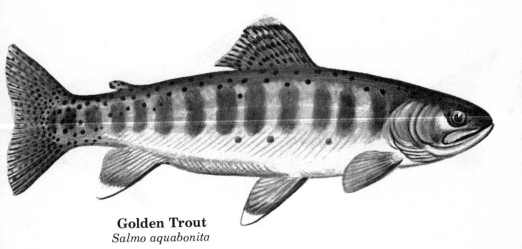

Golden Trout
Salmo aquabonita

Burbot
Lota lota

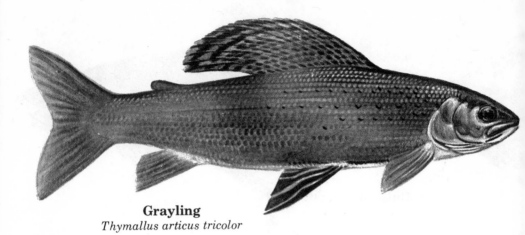

Grayling
Thymallus articus tricolor

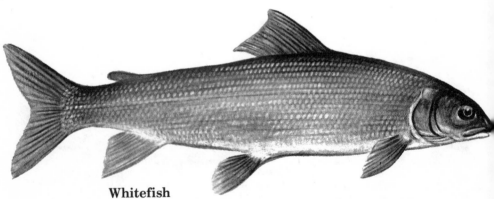

Lake Trout
Salvelinus namaycush

Whitefish
Prosopium williamsoni

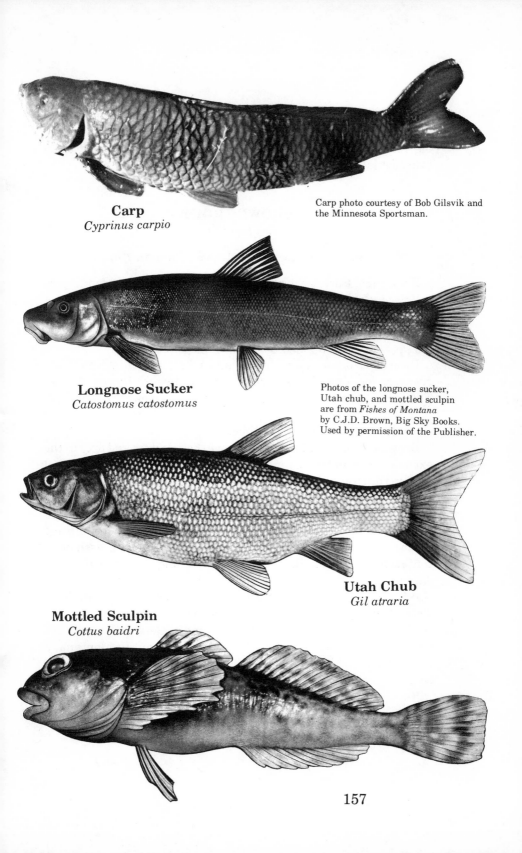

Carp
Cyprinus carpio

Carp photo courtesy of Bob Gilsvik and the Minnesota Sportsman.

Longnose Sucker
Catostomus catostomus

Photos of the longnose sucker, Utah chub, and mottled sculpin are from *Fishes of Montana* by C.J.D. Brown, Big Sky Books. Used by permission of the Publisher.

Utah Chub
Gil atraria

Mottled Sculpin
Cottus baidri

relatives in the Missouri drainage are lake trout. Brookies are an exotic fish, introduced into Montana waters in 1889, with debatable results. They compete too well with other trout, and often overpopulate and stunt.

BROWN TROUT
Salmo trutta

(Local names: Lock Leven, Lock, German Brown)

Brown trout are most easily identified by a rich golden to pale yellow side, with brilliant red to pink spots surrounded by halos of gray to pink. Small scales will be apparent (brook trout, the most likely candidate for confusion, appear to have no scales, and their red spots are surrounded by halos of blue).

Brown trout are found in lowland lakes, and in streams and rivers or sections of rivers with moderate-to-slow flow velocities. The largest brown trout recorded in Montana was 29½ pounds. A 16-inch fish is a good catch, but browns in the four to eight pound class do not make local headlines.

Browns, especially large browns, can be selective and foxy in the extreme. A seventeen pound specimen was shocked up from a local stream rumored to be fished out. Generally, browns in excess of the 16-inch median are taken on bait in the spring, or on a large lure or sculpin imitation like the muddler in midsummer and the fall. Browns under sixteen inches most commonly fall prey to an insect imitation: a dry, a wet, or a nymph. Working a large grasshopper imitation into the bank is a stand-out technique in late July and August.

Brown trout are an exotic fish, introduced into the Madison River drainage in 1889. Local anglers sometimes claim that there is a difference between a "Lock Leven" and a "German Brown," but there is no taxonomic support for the contention. In Montana, a brown trout is a brown trout, and by any other name they are the same.

158

CUTTHROAT TROUT
Salmo clarki

(Local names: Cutt, Native,
Yellowstone Cutthroat, Spotted Trout)

The bright red slashes on either side of the underside of the jaw is one characteristic of the cutthroat and the source of its name. Although cutthroat readily and frequently hybridize with rainbow trout, these red slashes remain dominant. Look, too, for round black spots on their side and top fins (rainbow have irregularly-edged black spots). Pure cutthroat also have pinkish gill plates, and the color fades to gray, then golden brown as you move toward the anal fin. If these latter characteristics are absent, especially the round spots, but if the red slashes are present on the throat, you probably have caught a hybrid, known locally as a cuttbow.

Cutthroat trout are common in the uppermost reaches of the Missouri headwaters and in alpine lakes in the region. The largest recorded specimen was sixteen pounds, but 14-inches rates as a respectable catch. Cutts have a decided preference for insect imitations, especially sub-surface forms, and in lake environments they feed heavily on scuds and snails. This latter diet produces a rich, pink flesh that has a superb flavor.

The cutthroat trout is native to the region and was first reported by the Lewis and Clark Expedition (1803-06). At that time these fish populated the Missouri north to Great Falls, but their range decreased with the advent of logging and farming, and their attendant pollution.

GOLDEN TROUT
Salmo aquabonita

(Local name: Goldens)

Golden trout are most readily identified by a golden side, cut by a bright scarlet lateral stripe. Their spotting (black, round) is most prominant along the back, behind the dorsal fin. Mature adults sport a scarlet underside from their jaw to the anal fin, and most fish retain parr marks (faint oblong stripes at right angles to the lateral line) throughout their life.

Goldens are almost exclusively high mountain lake fish, so the likelihood of hooking one in the Missouri's larger tributaries is slim. Major fisheries lie in the Portal Creek drainage of the Gallatin, and in the Beartooth Plateau, which drains into the Yellowstone.

Golden trout are insect oriented, and small insects at that. Midges and caddis flies, and small terrestrials on a #16 to #20 hook are recommended. The largest golden trout I have heard taken from Montana waters was nine pounds. 15-inches is a most respectable fish, and to snare that size, plan on working your way up through a lot of 7- and 8-inch lightweights. It is worth the effort, however, if only to witness the striking beauty of this trout and its environment. Goldens are native to the Kerr River drainage of California. They were introduced into Montana in 1907.

LAKE TROUT
Salvelinus namaycush

(Local names: Laker, Mack, Mackinaw)

Lake trout only inhabit lakes, one clue to winnowing out the species. Furthermore, Elk Lake, near West Yellowstone, and the Twin Lakes, southwest of Wisdom, are the only lakes in the Upper Missouri drainage where you'll find them. Other definitive characteristics include a dark gray back, and a light gray side with numerous light gray spots. Their belly is light gray to white, and they resemble a washed-out brook trout in body structure, with the exception of a deeply-forked tail. The tail on a brookie is nearly square.

The lakers in Elk and Twin Lakes are a true native population. They are primarily fish-eaters that are most commonly taken by deep trolling methods. In the spring and fall, just before and after ice out, they can be taken from shallows with spinning or fly equipment and an imitation or natural minnow. A 2½- to 3-pound laker rates as an average fish. The lake trout is not a true trout; it is a char.

RAINBOW TROUT
Salmo gairdneri

(Local names: Bow, Silver Salmon)

The most prominent marking on a rainbow is the pink to red stripe which runs from gill plate to tail along the lateral line. On small specimens and on fish taken from very clear lakes, the color may be faint; in this case, their backs will appear blue to green, their sides silver — hence the local misnomer "silver salmon." Rainbows have a blunter head than either browns or cutthroat, and specimens under twelve inches have a larger eye and a smaller, daintier mouth. Their teeth are much smaller than those of an equivalent-sized brown, and rainbows have irregularly-edged black spots on the back, upper fins, and side. Cutthroat have round, black spots.

Rainbows seek out fast, well-oxygenated stretches of streams and rivers, and they thrive in lake environments. They are found throughout the headwaters of the Missouri, and the largest 'bow taken in the area was 19½-pounds. A 15-incher is a nice fish.

Although they occasionally fall prey to a natural or imitation minnow, rainbows are primarily insect-oriented and given to violent, spectacular leaps. I've taken a few photographs of these fish in the air; they don't just jump — they vibrate, and their outline is a blur at shutter speeds under 1/500th of a second.

The rainbow is native to the western slopes of Montana's Continental Divide, having been introduced to the eastern slopes in 1889. This species frequently crosses with cutthroat trout producing a hybrid known as a cuttbow.

GRAYLING
Thymallus articus tricolor

(Local names: Gray Trout, White Trout)

Grayling are marked by a sail-like dorsal fin. They are irregularly spotted on their back and have a brownish-gray stripe on either side of their whitish underbelly. Large grayling sport blue, green, and pink irridescent striping on their dorsal fin; and pink striping on their pectoral, caudal, and anal fins. Grayling have

161

small teeth. All these features distinguish them from whitefish, which they otherwise resemble, with small mouths, an adipose fin, large scales, and a deeply forked tail.

Grayling are generally restricted to lakes and headwater streams and rivers at higher elevations. They are spring spawners, and their eggs are highly sensitive to the effects of siltation; hence their habitat must remain relatively clear during run-off. These fish have a strong preference for flies. In fact, it's a minor rarity to catch one on a spoon, minnow, or worm. Gray wet flies or nymphs like the Hare's Ear pattern pack special appeal.

Grayling are native to the Missouri headwaters, which has the largest fishery for this species in the lower 48. Like the cutthroat, another native, their range once extended to the Great Falls of the Missouri.

The largest grayling caught in Montana weighed two and a half pounds. A 14-incher rates as a mountable fish.

WHITEFISH
Prosopium williamsoni

(Local name: Mountain Whitefish)

If you catch a lot of them on flies and they have obvious scales, you're probably looking at whitefish. Beyond that observation, whitefish have a grayish to brownish back, silvery sides, and a whitish belly, with no black markings or spots. They have an adipose fin (the small fatty, meaty fin between the dorsal and the tail that is found on trout as well) and a small mouth with no teeth. Large males look bottle-nosed.

Whitefish inhabit all the Missouri headwaters, with the exception of lakes and fast streams at high elevations. You may even find them in lakes, but they like to stay near inlet streams, where there is moving water. Aquatic insects are the preferred diet of this species, and huge schools of whitefish often assemble in riffles at the heads of holes, boiling the water with their feeding activities.

A 12-inch whitefish is average. A 4-pounder is huge. Whitefish make excellent eating, especially when they're taken from cold water, or in the winter. They are especially good smoked. Although some anglers look on this species as a trash fish, they are strong fighters and most endearing, perpetually cooperative. When trout turn off, you can always find some willing whitefish to amuse you.

Whitefish are native to the headwaters of the Missouri.

BURBOT
Lota lota

(Local names: Ling, Ling Cod)

The ling looks like a cross between a catfish and an eel, with a flat, broad head, one set of whiskers, and a skinny, elongated tail adorned with long dorsal and anal fins. Scales will not be apparent, and their back appears to be marbled dark brown to olive.

Ling are abundant on the lower reaches of the Missouri headwaters, but they are seldom caught by fishermen, owing to their preference for natural bait, deep holes, and winter and nighttime feeding habits. Two pounds is an average fish; ten pounds is large.

If you've never seen a ling, pulling one out of the water will be a sobering experience. They look fearful, but they're harmless, and they are one of the best-eating fish that swims. Burbot are members of the codfish family and native to Montana.

ROUGH FISH

CARP
Cyprinus carpio

(Local names: German Carp, Mirror Carp, Leather Carp)

Carp have a compressed, husky-looking body, and a smooth, round mouth adorned by short "whiskers" or barbels. Their coloration ranges from gray to brown on their back, and pale yellow to rich golden on their sides. Their tail is deeply forked. German carp have large, regular scales; mirror carp have only a few large, irregular scales, and leather carp have no scales.

Carp are most common in the sluggish backwaters of the lower reaches of the Missouri drainage. They prefer natural baits, but they will occasionally take a fly. I have caught one on a lure.

Carp often feed on top, slurping down the surface film like pigs feeding on whey. When they head/tail, anglers often mistake them for feeding brown trout because of their golden hue. Carp average three to five pounds, and twenty pounds is a large fish.

Carp are an exotic, introduced into the region from Germany in 1886, and with much ado. One hundred years ago, carp were considered the kings of gamefish, and extensive plantings were made in this nation and abroad. It has since proved to be one of the greatest disasters in angling history.

SUCKER FAMILY
Catostomus...
catostomus (Longnose Sucker);
commersoni (White Sucker);
platyrhynchus (Mountain Sucker)

Suckers are distinguished by a round, toothless suction cup-like mouth beneath a rounded snub nose. Their body is slender and nearly cylindrical, with prominent scales, and their head appears flattened.

Suckers are common throughout the Missouri drainage, with the exception of the higher, swifter streams. They favor sluggish backwaters and deep holes, where they root about the bottom like mini-vacuum cleaners.

They are usually taken on bait, though I have hooked several on a fly.

CHUBS
Gil atraria (Utah Chub)
Hybopsis gracilis (Flathead Chub)
Couesius plumbeus (Lake Chub)

Chubs have a plumpish body covered with obvious scales, and no adipose fin; these characteristics quickly distinguish them from whitefish, which they resemble somewhat. Chub are also considerably smaller than the whitefish. An 8-inch chub is considered large.

164

They favor the slower sections of streams and abound in some area lakes. They prefer an insect diet, and are often taken on small flies.

MOTTLED SCULPIN
Cottus baidri

(Local names: Cottus, Bullhead, Baby Bullhead)

Sculpin strongly resemble a small bullhead, the feature from which their common name is derived. They have a broad, flat head, and a broad body, which tapers sharply toward the tail. Their color ranges from dark to olive brown on the back, and yellow to whitish on the belly. They have a long dorsal and anal fin, and a large mouth and eye. They seldom exceed four inches.

Sculpin are a major forage fish for game species, important to the fisherman in that they are the only legal minnow bait in the Missouri headwaters. This law prevents the introduction of rough or competitive species into pristine waters by way of escaped bait-fish. Sculpin are native to the area, in environmental tune with area rivers, streams, and lakes.

Sculpin are most commonly caught with a piece of window screening stretched between two sticks. One angler holds the screen while another herds sculpin into it, by walking roughly across the stream bottom. Sculpin prefer shallow riffles. The Muddler Minnow, one of the most popular and effective flies of the Missouri headwaters, is the artificial counterpart of the sculpin.

Maps & Resource Materials

Good maps are as important a piece of fishing gear as a Royal Coachman or felt soles on your waders. There are several sources of outstanding maps of the Missouri headwaters.

Bureau of Land Management (BLM)

Montana State Office
Granite Towers
Box 30157
Billings, MT 59101

Dillon District Office
Ibey Building
P.O. Box 1048
Dillon, MT 59726

BLM maps, tilted "National Resource Lands in Montana," incorporate excellent details, though no contour lines. Aside from major landmarks and geographical features, these maps are color-coded and delineate all parcels of State and Federal lands. They offer invaluable help when you are looking for access to a river, or for a patch of ground to camp on for a night. They cost 50¢ each.

BLM maps are keyed to a grid of Montana.

#31: Big Hole — includes the upper Big Hole River from Wise River to its headwaters.

166

#32: Dillon — includes the Big Hole from Wise River to Twin Bridges, the Beaverhead in its entirety, and the Jefferson, from Twin Bridges to Whitehall.

#33: Madison — includes the Jefferson from Whitehall to the Three Forks the Madison from Wall Creek to the Three Forks, and the entire Gallatin River outside Yellowstone National Park.

#34: Park — maps the Yellowstone from Yellowstone Park to Big Timber.

Montana Recreation Guide

Montana Dept. of Fish, Wildlife
  and Parks
1420 E. 6th Ave.
Helena, MT 59601

This guide is a map of state parks, state monuments, recreation areas, and fishing access sites. It lists the facilities available at each place and has written directions that tell you how to get there. As a map, it isn't much, and I have found a few mistakes in the mileposts, so if you follow them to the letter and still can't find the access, ask directions.

Its listings are helpful, though, especially when used in conjunction with another, more detailed map. And besides, you can't beat the price; it's free.

U.S. Dept. of Agriculture, Forest Service Visitors Map

U.S. Dept. of Agriculture
Forest Sevice
14th & Jefferson Dr. SW
Washington, DC 20250

Beaverhead National Forest
Box 1258
Dillon, MT 59725

Deerlodge National Forest
Federal Building, Box 400
Butte, MT 59701

Gallatin National Forest
Federal Building, Box 130
Bozeman, MT 59715

Helena National Forest
Steamboat Block Building
616 Helena Ave.
Helena, MT 59601

Forest Sevice Visitor Maps are comparable to BLM maps in that they have no contours and plainly identify land ownership. They are larger and more unwieldy, but they include one important feature that BLM maps lack, a key to the U.S. Geodetic Survey contour maps of the region. The Deer Lodge National Forest maps include the Jefferson from the Lewis and Clark Caverns to Twin Bridges; and the Big Hole from near Glen to Dickey Bridge.

The Beaverhead Forest map includes the Upper Big Hole, the Big Hole below Glen, the Beaverhead River, and part of the Madison.

The Gallatin National Forest map includes the Gallatin River, the Three Forks area, and the Missouri.

U.S. Geological Survey Maps

U.S. Geological Survey
Denver Distribution Center Federal Center, Building 41
Denver, Colorado 80225

These are contour maps, with exquisite detail. If you are considering a trip into the back country, they are a must, for they reveal the pitch of a climb and other terrain features from which you can orient yourself. The easiest way to identify the contour maps you'll need for your trip is via a Forest Visitors map of the area. The Visitors maps have a gridded key to the names of the contour maps of the region. Without that key, you'll have a difficult time nailing down just what map it is you want.

The Montanans' Fishing Guide: East

Mountain Press Publishing Co.
P.O. Box 2399
Missoula, MT 59806

This book, by Dick Konizeski, is an exhaustive review of every lake, river, and stream on the East slopes of the Continental Divide. It tells you how to get to your goal, what the roads are like, the water conditions you'll encounter, and the size and variety of the fish you'll catch. If you want to venture beyond the limits of the major streams and popular lakes, this book is a must.

Fishing Knots

Improved Clinch Knot

Use this knot to tie terminal tackle to your line or leader end. If the eye of the hook, lure, or snapswivel you're tying on to is large enough, go through it twice. This cushions line against line and pits abrasion against two points rather than one. On small flies, going through the eye twice will be difficulty, if not impossible. Go through once and check your knot strength often.

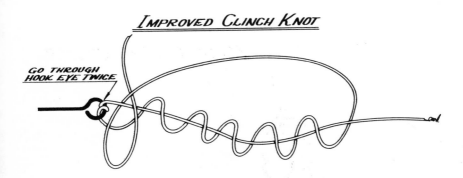

IMPROVED CLINCH KNOT

GO THROUGH
HOOK EYE TWICE

Nail Knot

The nail knot is the best of its breed for connecting leader and backing to the ends of your fly line. It doesn't make a splash when it settles down on the water, and it will not jam in a snake guide when you fight a fish down into the leader, or off your backing.

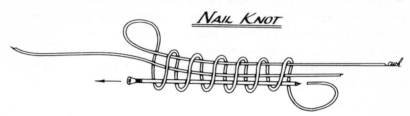

Blood Knot and Dropper

The blood knot is the standard for connecting leaders and tippets. If you want to work a fly on a dropper, tie a blood knot so that one of the tag ends of the two lines joined will be six- to nine-inches long when the knot is snugged up tight. Tie your dropper fly to it.

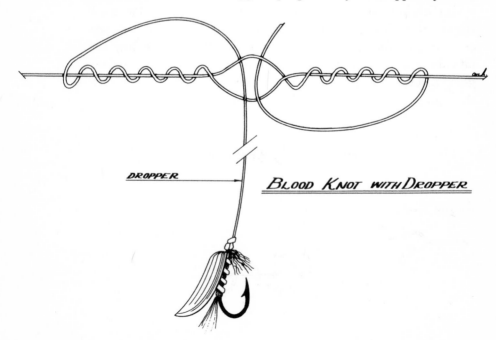

170

APPROXIMATE GROWTH RATE OF
OF MISSOURI HEADWATER GAME FISH
(Inches)

	Years					
	1	2	3	4	5	6
Brook	3	6	8	10	12	—
Brown	4	8	12	14	16	18
Cutthroat	3	6	8	10	12	—
Golden	6	12	15	16	—	—
Grayling	5	9	12	13	14	—
Lake Trout	3	6	9	14	20	25
Rainbow	3	8	11	13	16	18
Whitefish	4	8	11	13	14	16

Temperature Profile
of the Madison

Use this temperature profile to determine what hatches may be due and what the relative activity of feeding periods is.

In general, the Big Hole, Beaverhead, Jefferson, and Missouri follow these patterns closely. The Gallatin and Yellowstone run slightly cooler in the summer.

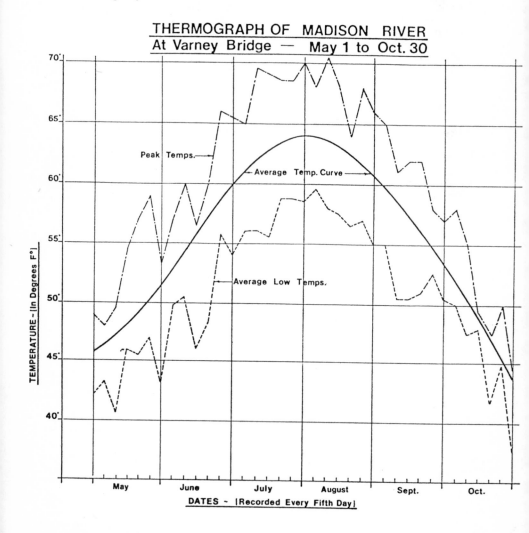

THERMOGRAPH OF MADISON RIVER
At Varney Bridge — May 1 to Oct. 30

HELP PRESERVE
THE FISHING ON THE
MISSOURI HEADWATERS

...and across the nation – by joining Trout Unlimited.

This non-profit organization is dedicated to one goal: the conservation and enhancement of trout stocks, and their habitat, in America.

For further information write:

**Trout Unlimited
4260 E. Evans Ave.
Denver, CO 80222**

OTHER BOOKS BY THE AUTHOR

FISHING

The Fisherman's Almanac
When, where, and how to catch fresh and salt water fish across America. (Hardback) $5.95

Spinfishing
Spinning tackle and tactics in fresh and salt water for all gamefish. (Hardback) $14.95 (Softback) $8.95

To Catch A Trout
Join the author for a day's fishing on a mythical river. (Hardback) $10.95

HUNTING

The Complete Hunter's Catalog
A showcase of equipment, information, and fact about 1000 products for the nimrod. (Softback) $8.95

The Hunter's Almanac
When, where, and how to hunt America's big and small game, waterfowl, and varmints. (Hardback) $5.95

Deer Hunting
Tactics and equipment for all North American deer. (Softback) $6.95

Misty Mornings and Moonless Nights
A waterfowler's handbook. Includes tactics, decoy patterns, and equipment. (Hardback) $9.95

GENERAL OUTDOORS

Whitewater!
Running America's rivers by raft, canoe, and kayak. (Hardback) $14.95 (Softback) $7.95

These books may be purchased from:
COTTONWOOD BOOKS
13830 Cottonwood Canyon
Bozeman, Montana 59715